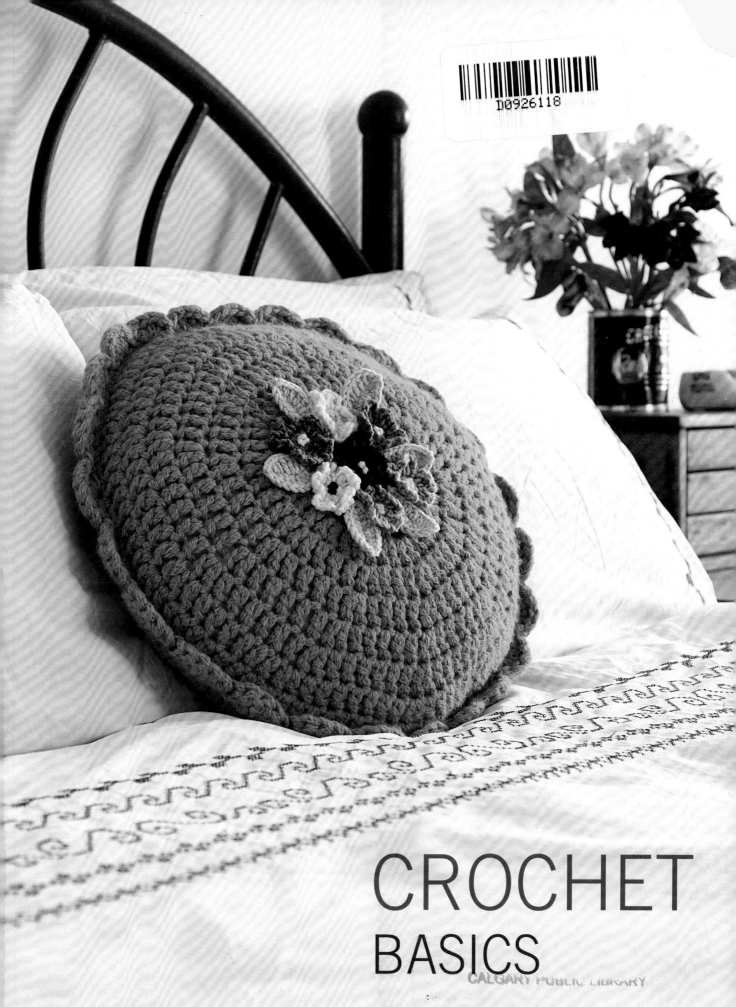

CROCHET
BASICS

CROCHET
BASICS

A step-by-step course for first-time stitchers

Nicki Trench

CICO BOOKS

LONDON NEW YORK

Published in 2014 by CICO Books
an imprint of Ryland Peters & Small
341 E 116th St
New York
NY 10029

www.rylandpeters.com

10 9 8 7 6 5 4 3 2 1

A CIP catalog record for this book is available
from the Library of Congress.

US ISBN 978 1 78249 150 7

Printed in China

Editors: Marie Clayton and Sally Harding
Design: Barbara Zuniga
Photography: James Gardiner (photographs on
pages 121 and 123: Emma Mitchell)
Stylist: Jo Thornhill
Still-life photography: Martin Norris
Step-by-step artworks: Stephen Dew
Chart artworks: Emily Breen and Kuo Kang Chen
Pattern checkers: Susan Horan, Sally Harding,
and Jane Czaja

Managing editor: Gillian Haslam
In-house designer: Fahema Khanam
Art director: Sally Powell
Production controller: Sarah Kulasek-Boyd
Publishing manager: Penny Craig
Publisher: Cindy Richards

Contents

Introduction

Although once thought of as old-fashioned and dated, crochet has now definitely turned the corner to become a fashionable and amazingly popular craft. The revival and popularity of all things "vintage" and homemade has had a lot to do with this, but it's also because of the huge range of colors in soft yarns that are now available. And so easily available! You no longer have to rely on a little wool shop on the corner of the high street that may or may not still be there—you can now order all the yarns you need over the Internet from the comfort of your own home or during your lunch break.

Crochet is also being used by top designers, who are coming back to the idea of using the wonderful variety of color and texture that only crochet can offer. Basically, it's everywhere, in both fashion and home textiles, and it's now giving knitting and sewing a good run for their money.

I've been teaching crochet in my workshops for several years now and the thing I love about it is that it crosses all generations. I'm finding a lot of younger people coming along, many of whom have heavyweight jobs and need to do something creative and relaxing away from the harshness of hard drives and hard-hitting deals.

In this book, I've brought together all the information I've gathered over the years for my crochet workshop students. I've broken down the essential techniques of crochet into small step-by-step chunks that are explained in minute detail. I've also designed some great projects for you to practice your techniques—not just for the sake of practicing, but also in the hope that you'll love the designs and want to make them so much you won't be able to put your hook down.

The great thing about crochet is that it's so portable. If I'm traveling anywhere I will take a small bag just big enough for a ball or two of yarn, a crochet hook and some scissors and then I'm off! Easy to whip out in waiting rooms or on buses and no fear of hitting the person sitting next to me with long knitting needles. The only downside is the trail of cut threads that I leave on seats and platforms from snipping off my sewn-in thread ends.

Please use this book as your crochet "bible" and it will set you up with a very satisfying and addictive skill for life.

How to use this book

Section 1: Getting Started

In this first part of the book you find everything you need to know about the basics of crochet. There are so many yarns available that sometimes you can be baffled by what they all are or are used for, but in this section we explain how to read the ball band and decipher the information given, and the differences between the most common thicknesses of yarns. You only need basic equipment for crochet so we have also listed some of the essentials with useful tips about all the items to get you started.

Following this are instructions and illustrations about how to hold the hook and yarn, how to make the basic stitches and explaining exactly where and how to place your hook, as well as the angle at which you should hold the hook at all stages. Finally there is also information on how to read a pattern, common abbreviations, and how to care for your crochet, yarns, and equipment.

Once you've practiced and mastered the basic stitches and techniques covered in this section you will feel confident enough to go on to the Workshops and Patterns Section.

Section 2: Workshops and Patterns

There are 20 Workshops in this section, with each Workshop covering in full step-by-step detail the stitches and techniques that you need to allow you to progress to the next level. Each Workshop also has a pattern for a project that fits in with the level of stitches and techniques that have been covered by the time you reach that stage. If you are a complete beginner, work consecutively through each Workshop, starting at Workshop 1. If you have already mastered some of the stitches, you can choose a Workshop that suits your own skill level.

I've tried to design projects that will appeal to all, so please use this book simply for the designs and patterns if you're already a competent crocheter. Sometimes the simple designs are the best!

Section 1
Getting Started

Getting Started

To get started on your new passion for crochet, you'll need some essential tools and tips. It can be very daunting to know what yarn and hooks to buy and how to start off holding your yarn, making your first stitches and reading a pattern. Please use this section as a guide—it will give you all the basic information you need with detailed step-by-step instructions.

Yarns

Of the masses of yarns that are available, the ones that are particularly easy to crochet with are yarns that are more tightly spun—which means the strands won't split apart. Modern yarns are generally "soft" yarns and by their nature they are quite loosely spun. You'll want to crochet with them, of course, so the trick is to practice the techniques, while making sure that you don't crochet too tightly. If your loops are slightly looser, when you draw the yarn through there is less chance of it catching in the hook and splitting. My favorite "soft" yarns to crochet with are fingering (4-ply), light worsted (DK), or worsted (aran) weights in flat colors. With these it is easier to count stitches and there are many beautiful color ranges and soft textures available.

Standard Yarn Weight
Categories of yarn, gauge ranges and recommended needle and hook sizes

Yarn weight symbol & category names	LACE 0	SUPER FINE 1	FINE 2	LIGHT 3	MEDIUM 4	BULKY 5	SUPER BULKY 6
Types of yarns** in category	10-count crochet thread, US fingering	UK 4-ply sock, baby, US fingering	baby, US sport	DK, US light worsted	US worsted, afghan, Aran	craft, rug, chunky	bulky, roving, UK super chunky
Recommended hook in metric size range	1.6–2.25 mm	2.25–3.5 mm	3.5–4.5 mm	4.5–5.5 mm	5.5–6.5 mm	6.5–9 mm	9 mm and larger
Recommended hook US size range	6, 7, 8 steels, B-1	B-1 to E-4	E-4 to 7	7 to I-9	I–9 to K–10½	K-10½ to M-13	M-13 and larger

** The generic yarn-weight names in the yarn categories include those commonly used in the UK and US.
Ultra-fine lace-weight yarns are difficult to put into gauge ranges; always follow the gauge given in your pattern for these yarns.

My choice of colors varies. At the moment I'm really keen on the Nordic colors that are around—blues or pinks with highlights of orange or red. There are some wonderful colors out there and the great thing about crochet is how easy it is to use color. If you're not confident in choosing color, don't worry—my advice is to always go with something you love and take it from there.

If you are starting out in crochet, be aware that there are some yarns that are more difficult to crochet with and some that are pretty unsuitable for crochet. There are many "fancy" yarns available on the market. These are usually fashion yarns and they are spun in a non-uniform way, so you may have strands of thick and thin yarn with perhaps a sparkle of lurex or beads spun into the strands. This type of yarn is more difficult to crochet with than a smooth yarn. With crochet, you are just working on one loop on the hook and the hook has to be able to go through this loop easily and smoothly; strands of non-uniform thicknesses will make loops that vary in size so you may be trying to pull a thick bit of the yarn through a small loop made from the thin bit of the yarn—beware! Stay away from bouclé yarn as well. It is spun with loops along the strand—very difficult to crochet with and you'll want to give up.

Some non-smooth yarns are worth the effort. For example, mohair and fluffy yarns are difficult but not impossible to crochet with and they create beautiful crochet textures as you can see in the Mohair Scarf on page 114. But mohair is not for the faint-hearted—it is difficult to undo, so I recommend that you practice a stitch or motif first using a smooth double knitting or Aran yarn to make yourself familiar with the technique. It's also best when crocheting in mohair to crochet very loosely.

Different types of yarn

There are a huge variety of yarns to choose from with all different types of fibers. Here are some of the more common types:

The naturals
100% wool
If a yarn is marked as "100% wool," this means that it has 100% animal content of some kind, usually sheep. If the ball band says merino, this comes from the Merino breed of sheep, well known for its fine soft fiber content. Other breeds of sheep also produce soft yarns, for example Blue Faced Leicester, which is a British breed.

Alpaca
Alpaca yarns are mainly mixed with merino yarns, typically 50:50. Alpaca is a natural fiber that comes from the animal of the same name. Depending on how it is spun, alpaca yarn can be either heavy or light and is available in a variety of thicknesses. It is soft, warmer than sheep's wool and has no lanolin, which makes it hypoallergenic.

Cashmere
A very soft and silky fiber, which comes from the undercoat of goats and is a hair rather than a fleece. It's a very warm and fine fiber usually spun into a fine yarn. Cashmere is often used in a mix with wool because a ball of 100% cashmere yarn is very expensive.

Cotton
A natural fiber, cotton comes in all thicknesses, starting with the finest threads. It was very popular in crochet several years ago when crocheters used the finely spun cottons for garments and home accessories. Recently produced cottons are spun considerably thicker and are often good for summer projects. Cotton is often mixed with acrylics and wool, which make it into a softer yarn.

Mohair
Mohair is a "hairy," silky fiber that is made from the hair of the Angora goat. It is often used with a mix of silk and wool. It dyes very well and the colors are often vibrant. It's more expensive than wool fibers and is spun fine, although the long hair fibers crochet as a dense and warm fabric and can be used with a comparatively thick hook.

Bamboo
Bamboo yarn is a very soft yarn and is produced, as its name implies, from bamboo fibers. It's often mixed with cotton or with other fibers.

The synthetics
Acrylic
Acrylic yarn is synthetic and is manufactured to imitate wool yarn. Its appeal is that it is a cheaper fiber than wool. It is often mixed with wool to create a more economic yarn, while retaining some of the warmth properties of pure wool. Aside from the cost advantage, the other advantage is that many acrylic yarns can be put in the washing machine.

Fancy yarns
"Fancy" yarn is a general term and it covers anything that might be fashionable. Fancy yarns are generally made of a mix of acrylics and can be "hairy" with a touch of shimmer from added lurex, sequins, or glitter.

There are also ribbon yarns, which are fabric strips of ribbon that are wound into balls. These work best for crochet if they have a bit of stretch to them, and when crocheted they create an interesting and sometimes ruffled effect.

You can also buy balls of fabric strips. These are often used for large projects worked on an extra-large crochet hook—sometimes as thick as a broom handle. They are ideal for crocheting rugs and cushion seats.

"Fur" is another fancy yarn that is more commonly used in knitting—I don't recommend it for crocheting. The fibers of the fur are too long and the strands too difficult to pull through the loop on a crochet hook.

Balls and hanks of yarn

You'll find "balls" of yarn in either an oblong or doughnut shape. There is no particular reason why one is wound one way or the other—the yarn companies choose the way they want the manufacturer to present the "ball" for aesthetic purposes.

You will find one end of the yarn on the outside of the wound ball, this is the end that you should use. But you can also use the end from inside the ball if you like—I prefer not to use this end because the yarn tends to get more tangled.

A hank (or skein) of yarn has not been wound into a ball yet and is held together as a big loop of yarn. It needs to be wound into a ball before you begin to crochet—if you try to crochet straight from a hank the strands of yarn will soon become very tangled.

Yarn thicknesses

You can use any weight (or thickness) of yarn with crochet. Traditionally fine and laceweight yarns were used to make doilies and sofa back covers, but the fashion now is to use thicker and softer yarns for garments and accessories. I started out using quite chunky yarns; I liked how quickly they crocheted up, and the look of chunky scarves and hats. But now I appreciate finer work and usually work with worsted (DK) or fingering (4-ply) yarns.

For a beginner, the easiest yarn to learn with is a double knitting yarn or an aran-weight yarn, using a US size E-4 to I-9 (3.5 mm to 5.5 mm) crochet hook.

The stitches produced are around the right size to count easily and the hook size is comfortable.

Yarns are manufactured in a wide range of thicknesses, from fine laceweight yarns and cotton threads up to super chunky. The Standard Yarn-Weight System chart (see page 10) lists most of the standard weights available and classes them into generic groups. If you need to find a yarn substitute you need one with the same recommended hook size, as shown on the chart on page 10, and gauge (stitches per 4 in./10 cm), which will be indicated in the pattern itself.

Winding a ball

If you can find a willing person with two strong arms, drop the hank around their hands, with their thumbs held upward. Undo any strings or knots that tie the loop together before you start to wind the hank into a ball. If you can't find a willing person, put two chairs together back to back and drape the hank securely around the backs of the chairs. There are also commercial ball winders available and if you're having to wind lots of balls from hanks it might be worth purchasing one.

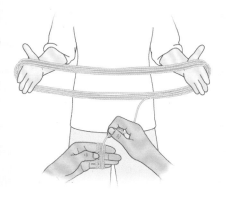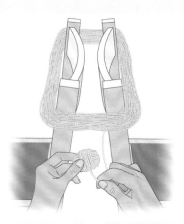

How to wind a ball of yarn from a hank

1 Start to wind one end of the yarn from the hank several times around your fingers.

2 Slide this "wrap" off your fingers, turn it and wind the yarn around the wrap in the other direction.

3 Continue to wind the yarn this way, intermittently turning the ball to wrap in a different direction, until the entire hank is wound onto the ball.

Understanding yarn labels

When buying yarn it will usually either be held together by a paper "ball band" or have a card label attached somewhere on the ball or hank. The label (or band) will have the following information about the yarn:

- **Yarn company** (or brand of the yarn) and yarn name.

- **Length and weight:** This explains how many ounces (grams) the ball weighs and how many yards (meters) are on the ball, for example 125yd (115m) per 1¾oz (50g). Balls are usually 1¾oz (50g), but may sometimes be ⅞oz (25g) or 3½oz (100g).

- **Washing instructions:** Washing symbols are usually included on the yarn label. Generally speaking it's best to hand wash pure wool. Some yarns can be washed in the washing machine on the wool wash cycle and I very occasionally wash my crochet on a wool wash, but I've learned the hard way—all it takes is a little flick of the dial and the next thing you know the washing machine cycle is on the hottest temperature and you end up with something felted that only the cat would be happy with. As crocheters we dedicate many long hours to our hobby and the last thing we want is for our handmade treasure to be ruined in an instant. However, if you're confident with your washing machine, make sure you have it on the coolest setting—or crochet a small test piece first and wash that to check it really doesn't shrink.

- **Recommended hook size:** On most yarn labels a recommended knitting needle size is given rather than a crochet hook size. But if there is a recommended hook size on the label, remember that this is only a recommendation. You should always follow the crochet hook size specified in your crochet pattern, because the sweater or accessory has been designed using this specific size for a reason. For instance, for the Textured Pillow Cover (page 58) in this book I used a chunky yarn and a lace stitch. I wanted the lace stitch to be less open and tighter to give a plumpness to the pillow cover, so I have recommended a smaller hook compared to the usual larger hook that is recommended on the ball band.

- **Gauge guide:** Gauge refers to the size of stitch a yarn will create. The recommended gauge given on the yarn label is usually a knitted gauge, and it will say how many rows by how many stitches are achieved using the size of needle on the ball band. (See more about Gauge on page 26.)

- **Fiber content:** The fiber content of the yarn may be a single fiber, such as 100% wool, or a mix of fibers, for example, 50% alpaca/50% merino wool.

- **Color number and name:** Yarn companies have their own codes for colors and this will be shown on the label, possibly along with a color name. Color names usually relate to the company's current fashion collection and the names don't necessarily describe the actual color accurately. It's best to use the shade number as a guide, because yarn companies will occasionally change the names. It should also be noted that yarn shades go out of fashion so yarn companies will often discontinue these shades. This can be done at any time, so the shades given in patterns are only recommended. If you can no longer buy the exact shade specified in the pattern choose another shade—yarn companies will usually bring in very similar shades to their new collections.

- **Dye lot number:** This number indicates which batch the yarn was dyed with. The color can vary considerably from lot to lot, so if you're making a one-color item it's best to make sure each ball of yarn has the same dye lot number. If you're working on a multi-colored item, which is common in crochet, it's less important to have the same dye lots. When ordering yarn on the internet or buying from a shop you will generally be given balls of one color from the same dye lot. If you are making a garment, it's a good idea to order an extra ball in the same dye lot, as the number of balls specified in a pattern is only a guide—you may use up more or less balls depending on your personal stitch gauge.

- **Made in:** Some companies will put where the yarn originates from, or a website address for the yarn company.

Cotton DK 100% cotton
125yd (115m) per 1¾ oz (50g)

22 sts and 30 rows per 4 in. (10 cm) over st st using US size 6 (4 mm) knitting needles.
705 Pale Blue – Dye lot 7836
Made in Turkey
www.wondayarns.com

Crochet hooks

Crochet hooks come in a variety of sizes and you'll be guided by the pattern and the thickness of yarn as to which size you need. If you are purchasing your first hook for practice, then use a light worsted (DK) weight yarn and a US size G-6 (4 mm) crochet hook, or a worsted (Aran) weight and a US size H-8 (5 mm) hook.

Historically crochet hooks were made of bone, steel, porcupine quill, or ivory. Modern hooks are made in bamboo, wood, aluminium, steel, casein, or plastic. Some have handles made of plastic and many have a flat piece around the center of the length of the hook which is a thumb guide.

Personally, I don't use bamboo hooks. I always use wooden knitting needles because I don't like the clicking of plastic ones, but the varnish on bamboo crochet hooks wears off after a while and they then catch on the yarn. My favorite hook is one with a round plastic handle and a steel hook, which is made by a German company who distribute throughout the world. I like to use hooks with a round comfortable plastic handle like this, and a long enough steel part for me to make big wraps for stitches such as 7-double clusters where you have to wrap lots of yarn around the hook. I also like the handles to be color coded, so there is a different color for each size.

Whichever type of hook you choose, it's important that it has a good smooth tip—for this reason alone it's worth buying one of the more expensive brands. Be sure to try out different brands to see which ones you like the best before making a purchase (see page 155 for where to buy hooks).

You'll have your hooks for life if you look after them carefully. I keep mine in a hook holder so that I don't lose them, or in an old-fashioned wooden pencil stand where they are easily accessible.

Parts of a crochet hook

A crochet hook is a simple tool that is shaped to fit nicely in the hand and glide easily in and out of the crochet loops. Not all hooks of the same size have exactly the same shape, but the most standard shape is shown here. Most hooks of this shape are usually made completely of plastic or of steel. They have a flat area near the hook end that is a guide for where to put your thumb.

Standard hook

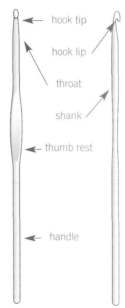

- hook tip
- hook lip
- throat
- shank
- thumb rest
- handle

A "comfort" hook has a handle made of plastic that is either round, flat, or oval-shaped, combined with a metal shank and hook.

Comfort hook

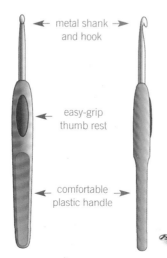

- metal shank and hook
- easy-grip thumb rest
- comfortable plastic handle

Crochet hook sizes

This chart shows how the modern metric sizes, the US sizes, and the old UK sizes relate to each other.

Metric sizes	US sizes	Old UK/ Canadian
1.25 mm	7 steel	
1.5 mm	6 steel	
1.75 mm	5 steel	
2 mm		14
2.25 mm	B-1	
2.5 mm		12
2.75 mm	C-2	
3 mm		11
3.25 mm	D-3	10
3.5 mm	E-4	9
3.75 mm	F-5	
4 mm	G-6	8
4.5 mm	7	7
5 mm	H-8	6
5.5 mm	I-9	5
6 mm	J-10	4
6.5 mm	K-10½	3
7 mm		2
8 mm	L-11	0
9 mm	M-13	00
10 mm	N-15	000
12 mm	P	
15 mm	Q (16 mm)	
20 mm	S (19 mm)	
25 mm	U	

Other equipment

It's important to have some basic equipment nearby when crocheting. The most important are scissors and a yarn sewing needle, but pins and a tape measure are also useful. I use small sharp embroidery scissors—my favorites have a ribbon tied onto the handle to make sure I can find them easily, which also shows the rest of the family that they are for my use only! I have an extra-long tape measure because I have to measure large blankets for my designs. But I have about ten other tape measures scattered around because I'm always putting them down and losing them.

Scissors
A small pair of sharp scissors is an essential tool for crocheters. Keep these separate from other scissors in the household and use them for yarn or thread only—never for paper because this will quickly blunt the blades.

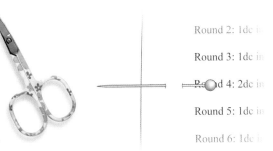

Round 2: 1dc i

Round 3: 1dc in

Round 4: 2dc in

Round 5: 1dc i

Round 6: 1dc i

Yarn sewing needles
Also called "darning needles," "wool needles," or "tapestry needles," yarn sewing needles are larger than ordinary sewing needles. They also have a bigger eye so you can thread yarns easily and some of them have blunt tips to avoid splitting the yarn. You'll need a yarn sewing needle for sewing in ends or sewing pieces of your crochet together. They come in different sizes so it's best to buy a few sizes to suit various yarn thicknesses. (See Sewing in Ends/Tails on page 24 for how to thread yarn into a yarn sewing needle.)

Tape measure
A tape measure is an inexpensive and a essential tool for a crocheter. You will need it to measure your crochet pieces and your gauge squares. It's handy to have one that has inches on one side and centimeters on the other.

Pattern-reading markers
It's really important to mark off where you are at the end of each round or row on your pattern. When you're trying out a new pattern, you should also mark the pattern stitch by stitch. I use a large plastic-headed pin to mark off my rounds/rows so my pieces of paper are covered in pin holes, but I find this easier to follow than pen or pencil marks. If you have a scanner or photocopier in your house, print off the pattern you're working on so you can write notes on it, make pen marks at the end of rows, or even "pin" it like I do.

Stitch markers
Stitch markers are essential for crocheters. If you're buying ready-made markers there are plastic, metal and even decorative ones—but be careful that the decorative ones don't have sharp edges to catch on the yarn.

I use stitch markers a lot in my crochet, but because I tend to lose the little shop-bought ones down the back of the sofa or armchair (they also get swallowed up by the vacuum cleaner and the dog), I use a piece of contrasting yarn about 4 in. (10 cm) long as a marker. You'll need markers to mark the beginning and end of a round when working in a spiral and for marking which is the wrong and right side of your work.

Curved safety pins, which are made for quilting, make great stitch markers. I use these to measure out lengths that need an edging. So if, for example, the pattern says to make 20 single crochet evenly along the edge, I mark the center of the length with the pin then I mark it into quarters so I can make five stitches evenly between each marker.

Pins
I always pin my crochet pieces together before I sew them up or make a crochet seam. Use big plastic or glass-headed pins for this so they don't get lost in the crochet. Also buy some standard dressmaking pins because these are useful when blocking—if you block using plastic-headed pins the heads may melt under the heat of the iron.

Storage equipment
Crocheters will always have scraps and left over balls of yarn. Yarn can sometimes catch on baskets so, although they look nice, they are not always the most practical solution for storage. Try plastic boxes or a workbag—I store my yarn in color-sorted plastic bags inside a plastic box. Be sure to wind up the strands so they don't get tangled or you will end up putting them in the bin because you can't untangle them.

Basic Stitches

Crochet has only a few basic stitches and once you've mastered these all
extended stitches follow the same principles. Practice the basic stitches before
attempting your first pattern. Crochet is easy to undo because you only have
one loop on the hook so you can't really go wrong. When practicing keep the
loops loose—you can work on creating an even gauge across the fabric later.

Holding your hook and yarn

Holding the yarn and hook
correctly is a very important part of
crochet and once you have practiced
this it will help you to create your
stitches at an even gauge.

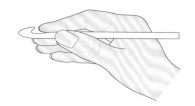

Holding your hook
There are two basic ways of holding the hook.
I always teach the pen position as I find this
more comfortable. It gives you a more relaxed
arm and shoulder.

Pen position Pick up your hook as though
you are picking up a pen or pencil. Keeping
the hook held loosely between your fingers
and thumb, turn the hook so that the tip is
facing up and the hook is balanced in your
hand and resting in the space between your
index finger and your thumb.

Knife position But if I'm using a very large
hook and chunky yarn, then I may sometimes
change and use the knife position. I crochet
a lot and I've learned that it's important to
take care not to damage your arm or shoulder
by being too tense. Make sure you're always
relaxed when crocheting and take breaks.

Holding your yarn
Pick up the yarn with your little finger on
the opposite hand to the hook, with palm
facing toward you, the short end in front
of the finger and the yarn in the crease
between little finger and ring finger. Turn
your hand to face downward (see right),
placing the long yarn strand on top of
your index finger, under the other two
fingers and wrapped right around the
little finger. Then turn your hand to face
you (far right), ready to hold the work in
your middle finger and thumb.

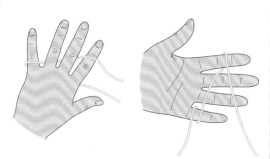

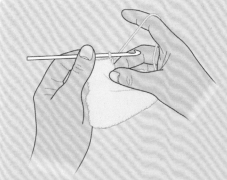

Holding hook and yarn while crocheting
Keep your index finger, with the yarn draped
over it, at a slight curve, and hold your work
(or the slip knot) using the same hand,
between your middle finger and your thumb
and just below the crochet hook and loop/s
on the hook.

   As you draw the loop through the hook
release the yarn on the index finger to allow
the loop to stay loose on the hook. If you tense
your index finger, the yarn will become too
tight and pull the loop on the hook too tight
for you to draw the yarn through.

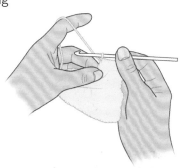

Holding hook and yarn for left-handers

Some left-handers learn to crochet like
right-handers, but others learn with
everything reversed—with the hook in
the left hand and the yarn in the right.

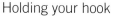

Slip knot

A slip knot is the loop that you put onto the hook to start any stitch in crochet.

1 Make a circle of yarn as shown.

2 In one hand hold the circle at the top where the yarn crosses, and let the tail drop down at the back so that it falls across the center of the loop. With your free hand or the tip of a crochet hook, pull a loop through the circle.

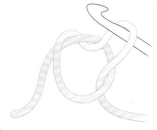

3 This forms a very loose loop on the hook.

4 Pull both yarn ends gently to tighten the loop around the crochet hook shank.

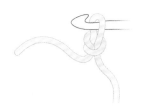

5 Make sure the loop is not TOO tight. It needs to slip easily along the shank.

Chain stitches (abbreviated ch)

Chains are the basis of all crochet. This is the stitch you have to practice first because you need to make a length of chains to be able to make the first row or round of any other stitch. Practicing these will also give you the chance to get used to holding the hook and the yarn correctly.

1 Start with the tip of the hook pointed upward, with the slip knot on your hook sitting loosely so there is enough gap to pull a strand of yarn through the loop on the hook.

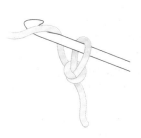

2 Catch the yarn with the hook, circling it around the strand of yarn.

Chain stitches in symbols

The chain is represented in a crochet chart (see page 26) by an oval. Each oval on the chart represents one chain.

3 As you catch the yarn, turn the tip of the hook downward, holding the knot immediately under the loop on the hook with your left hand between finger and thumb.

4 Then gently pull the strand of yarn through the loop on the hook. As soon as the tip of the hook comes through the loop, turn the tip of the hook immediately upward.

Foundation chain

A foundation chain is the length of chains that is made to start a straight piece of crochet. The first row of your stitches is worked into it. It's important always to begin with the correct number of foundation chains—if you don't, the rest of the pattern and stitches will not work. Crochet patterns are often worked in multiples and groups, so it's essential to learn how to count the chains.

Front of chain

The front of the chain (the right side) is the smooth side: each chain makes a little "V."

Back of chain

The back of the chain (the wrong side) is more bumpy, with little ridges.

Counting chains

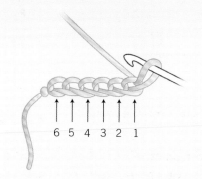

To count chains in a foundation chain, lay the chain out on a flat surface with the right side facing and count each "V" as one chain. Always count chains from the front of the chain (the end nearest to the hook) and do not count the loop on the hook as one chain.

Working into the foundation chain

When you start your first row in crochet, you will be instructed to crochet into the foundation chain. When making the stitches into a foundation chain, you'll be instructed to put the first stitch into the second, third or fourth chain from the hook, depending on the height of the stitches you'll be working with. This is usually in the second chain from the hook for single crochet, third chain from the hook for half doubles, or fourth chain from the hook for doubles. The loop that is on the hook is not counted. The first chain from the hook is the one that the loop is coming out of and you can't go into this, it will unravel.

Always follow the specific instructions given in the pattern. It may be that the rules of which stitch to go into differ according to the design.

How to work the first row into the foundation chain

Working into the foundation chain is always the most fiddly part of the crochet process. You don't have much to hold onto and it's important to keep the chain from twisting so that you're always working into the front of the chain.

To make the first stitch into your foundation chain, using the point of the tip of the hook and with the hook tilted slightly sideways, insert the hook into the middle of the chain, picking up the loop at the top of the chain.

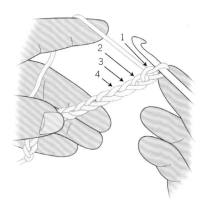

Turning chains

The turning chains are made at the beginning of a row (or round) of crochet. They are used to bring the hook up to the right height for the stitches you are going to work in that row. It will be indicated in the pattern whether these chains are counted as the first stitch or not. If your pattern instructions specify a different number of turning chains than the usual number given here, then always do as the pattern directs.

Single crochet:	1 turning chain
Half doubles:	2 turning chains
Double crochet:	3 turning chains
Trebles:	4 turning chains
Double trebles:	5 turning chains

Slip stitch (abbreviated ss)

A slip stitch is the shortest crochet stitch and is usually worked into other stitches rather than into a foundation chain, because it is rarely used to make a whole piece of crochet. It is mainly used to join rounds or to take the yarn neatly along the tops of stitches to get to a certain point without having to fasten off. It can also be used as a joining stitch (see Workshop 1, page 30).

Slip stitch in symbols

Each black dot on a crochet chart (see page 26) represents one slip stitch.

1 To make a slip stitch, first insert the hook through the stitch (chain or chain space). Then wrap the yarn round the hook.

2 Pull the yarn through both the stitch (chain or chain space) and the loop on the hook at the same time, so you will be left with one loop on the hook.

Single crochet (abbreviated sc)

Single crochet is the most commonly used stitch of all. It makes a firm tight crochet fabric. If you are just starting out, it is the best stitch to start with because it is the easiest to make.

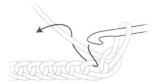   

1 Make a foundation chain, then insert the tip of the hook into the 2nd chain from the hook. Catch the yarn with the hook by taking the hook around the back of the yarn strand. Pull the yarn through the chain only with the hook pointed downward. As soon as you have brought the yarn through, immediately turn the hook upward—this will help to keep the loop on the hook and prevent it sliding off. Keep the hook in a horizontal position.

2 You will now have two loops on the hook. Wrap the yarn over the hook again (with the hook sitting at the front of the yarn), turn the hook to face downward and pull the yarn through the two loops, turning the hook to point upward as soon as you have pulled the yarn through.

3 One loop is now left on the hook. Keep the hook pointed upward (this is the default position of the hook until you start the next stitch). Continue working one single crochet into each chain to the end of the foundation chain.

4 Then turn the work to begin the next row. Make one chain and work the first single crochet into the top of the first single crochet in the row below (picking up the two loops at the top of the stitch). Work one single crochet into each single crochet stitch in the row below, to the end of the row.

5 For all subsequent rows, repeat Step 4.

Single crochet in symbols

Each oval on this chart represents one chain and the cross above the chain represents one single crochet stitch going into the chain. The chart is worked from the bottom to the top and the little black triangle represents where you start reading the chart from and the little triangle with a black outline represents the end. See page 26 for more information on charts.

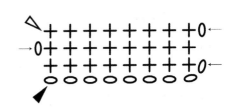

Half double crochet (abbreviated hdc)

Half doubles are stitches that are the next height up to a single crochet stitch. The yarn is wrapped over the hook first before going into the stitch (or space) and then once pulled through the stitch (or space) there will be three loops on the hook. The middle loop is from the strand that was wrapped over the hook. Before you attempt to pull the yarn through all three stitches, make sure the loops sit straight and loosely on the hook so that you can pull another strand through to complete the stitch.

1 Make your foundation chain as usual to start. Before inserting the hook into the work, wrap the yarn over the hook. Then with the yarn over the hook, insert the hook through the 3rd chain from the hook. Work "yarn over hook" again (as shown by the arrow).

2 Pull the yarn through the chain. You now have three loops on the hook. Yarn over hook again and pull it through all three loops on the hook.

3 You will be left with one loop on the hook. Continue working one half double into each chain to the end of the foundation chain.

— First half double of row

4 Then turn the work to begin the next row. Make two chains. Work one half double into each half double stitch in the row below to the end of the row.

5 For all subsequent rows, repeat Step 4.

Half double crochet in symbols

A half double crochet symbol on a crochet chart is a vertical line with a short horizontal line on the top like a "T." I always think of it having a little hat on the top. It's taller than a single crochet "cross" symbol, but not as tall as the double crochet symbol (see opposite) and this represents the size of the stitch in comparison to the others.

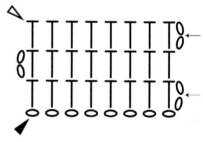

Double crochet (abbreviated dc)

A double crochet is a very common stitch; it gives a more open fabric than a single crochet or a half double, which both give a denser fabric, and it's a one step taller stitch than a half double. As with the half double, the yarn is wrapped over the hook first before going into the stitch (or space) and then once pulled through the stitch there are three loops on the hook. The middle loop is from the strand that was wrapped over the hook. Before you attempt to pull the yarn through the next two stitches on the hook, make sure the loops sit straight and loosely on the hook so that you can pull another strand through.

  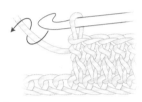

1 Before inserting the hook into the work, wrap the yarn over the hook. Then with the yarn wrapped over the hook, insert the hook through the 4th chain from the hook. Work "yarn over hook" again (as shown by the arrow).

2 Pull the yarn through the chain. You now have three loops on the hook. Yarn over hook again and pull it through the first two loops on the hook.

3 You now have two loops on the hook. Yarn over hook again and pull it through the two remaining loops.

4 You now have one loop on the hook. Continue working one double crochet into each chain to the end of the foundation chain.

— First st

5 Then turn the work to begin the next row. Make three chains. Work one double crochet into each double stitch in the row below to the end of the row.

6 For all subsequent rows, repeat Step 5.

Double crochet in symbols

The symbol for a double crochet on a chart is a vertical line with a short horizontal line at the top and with a diagonal short line crossed through the vertical line in the center. It's a taller symbol than the single crochet and half double crochet symbols, which represents the height of the stitch.

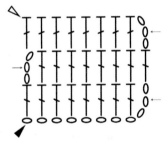

Increasing

You can increase by working two or three stitches into one stitch or space in the previous row. The illustration shows a two-stitch increase made in double crochet.

Decreasing

You can decrease by skipping the next stitch and continuing to crochet, or by crocheting two or more stitches together. The basic technique for crocheting stitches together is the same for all stitches. The following example shows single crochet 2 stitches together (sc2tog).

1 Insert the hook into the work, yarn over hook and pull through the work (two loops on hook), insert the hook in the next stitch, yarn over hook and pull the yarn through.

2 Yarn over hook again and pull through all three loops on the hook. You will then have one loop on the hook.

Basic techniques

The following techniques and tips cover the basic methods you need to know in order to make your first pieces of crochet, to follow a pattern and to finish off your projects.

Where to insert the hook in your crochet

One of the tricks of learning how to crochet is to understand clearly where to insert the hook to make a stitch, whether into a chain, a space in the crochet or into stitches in the row or round below. The general rule for working into the stitch below to make a new stitch is to pick up both the top loops of the stitch—that means you will usually be inserting your hook under the two loops at the top of the stitch that look like a "V." However, you may be instructed in the pattern to pick up either only the front or only the back loop, which gives the crochet a different "look" or texture.

Working into top of stitch

Unless otherwise directed the hook will be inserted into a stitch under both of the two loops on the top of the stitch. This is the standard technique.

Working into front loop of top of stitch

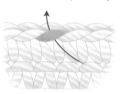

To pick up the front loop of the stitch, pick up the front loop from underneath at the front of the work.

Working into back loop of top of stitch

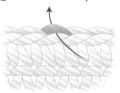

To pick up the back loop of the stitch, insert the hook between the front and the back loop, picking up the back loop from the front of the work.

How to measure a gauge square

Make a number of chains that measure to approximately 5–6 in. (13–15 cm) using the hook and the yarn recommended in the pattern. Make enough rows to form a square and then fasten off.

Take a tape measure or ruler, place it across your crocheted piece horizontally, and mark off the an area of 4 in. (10 cm) with pin markers. Count the number of stitches across 4 in. (10 cm), then take the tape measure/ruler and place it vertically and count the number of rows across 4 in. (10 cm). Compare the number of stitches

and rows you have counted to the gauge guide. If your rows and stitches measure the same as the guide, use this size hook and yarn to achieve the same gauge and measurements in the pattern. If you have more stitches, then your gauge is tighter than the sample and you need to use a larger crochet hook, if you have less stitches, then your gauge is looser and you'll need to use a smaller hook. Make gauge squares using different size hooks until you have reached the same gauge as the guide and then use this hook to make the project.

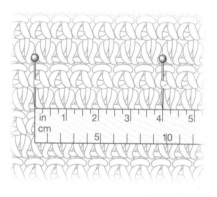

Measuring gauge

On most crochet patterns you'll find a gauge guide. This is usually the gauge that has been worked using the crochet hook size recommended and by the person who made the project. People work to different gauges: some are loose, some are tight and so it's important to achieve the right gauge to get the right measurements for your project. For example, if you are making a garment and the gauge guide is for a tighter

gauge than you crochet, then your garment will come out bigger than the measurements given.

Sometimes a gauge guide is not important, for example on flowers or some motifs because it's not really important if they turn out a little bigger or smaller. But if you are working on a garment or a pillow cover that has to finish to a particular measurement, then it's important to get it right.

Fastening off

Fastening off is important to stop the work from unraveling. You must cut the yarn first and then thread the tail through the loop. Pull the loop firmly and leave an end long enough to sew in the end afterward. An end of 4–6 in. (10–15 cm) is generally long enough, but make this the minimum length of tail—it may be best to leave ends slightly longer if using thick or chunky yarns.

To "cut off yarn"

You will be instructed to cut off (or break) the yarn if the work hasn't finished and a new color needs to be joined. When this instruction is given in your crochet pattern, do not fasten off the loop on your crochet hook. Simply cut the yarn at least 4 in. (10 cm) from the work and leave the loop on the hook. Then continue following the instructions for what to do next.

To "fasten off" a piece of crochet

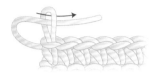

Cut the yarn, leaving a yarn tail of at least 4 in. (10 cm). Using the hook, pull the yarn tail all the way through the last loop and pull tightly.

Joining in a new ball of yarn

You may need to join a different ball of yarn when either the ball runs out or you need to bring in a new color. If joining when the ball runs out, try and join at the end of the row.

Joining at the end of a row/round

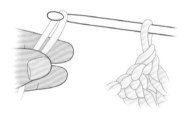

1 Keep the loop of the old yarn on the hook. Drop the tail and catch a loop of the strand of the new yarn with the crochet hook.

2 Pull the new yarn through the loop on the hook, keeping the old loop drawn tight.

Joining in the middle of a row

Sometimes you will need to join in a new yarn in the middle of the row, either because the yarn has run out and you need to use the same color but with a new ball, or when instructed in the pattern to change color. In this case you work part of the stitch in the old yarn and then switch to the new yarn to complete it, as explained in the instructions for joining on single crochet.

How to join in a new yarn on single crochet

Make a single crochet stitch as usual, but do not complete the stitch. When there are two loops remaining on the hook, drop the old yarn, catch the new yarn with the hook and pull it through these two loops to complete the stitch.

Continue to crochet with the new yarn. Cut the strand of the old yarn about 6 in. (15 cm) from the crochet and leave it to drop at the back of the work so you can sew this end in later.

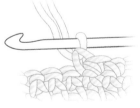

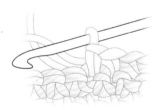

TIP

When changing yarns, if the strands of the new and old yarns are becoming loose, tie them together at the back of the work just once, to hold them in place. Do not make a double knot. You will weave in the ends later.

Sewing in yarn ends/tails

Sewing in yarn ends on your work is part of the crochet finishing process. In crochet you are often using a lot of different colors, so you'll be left with lots of ends. Sew in ends often as your work progresses, especially if you're making a large project such as a blanket. Consider it as part of the crochet and not a chore. Use the ends to neaten up the crochet and close center holes when making pieces in the round like motifs, flowers, and circles.

Threading a yarn needle
Use a yarn sewing needle when sewing in ends or sewing seams. Make sure the needle you have chosen has a large enough eye for the yarn to pass through it.

1 Hold an end of a yarn strand approx. 2 in. (5 cm) from the end.

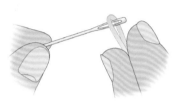

2 Make a small loop and place the end of the needle with the eye through the loop.

3 Pinch the loop tightly around the flat piece of the eye between your index finger and thumb.

4 Slide the needle out of the loop, keeping the yarn pinched tightly.

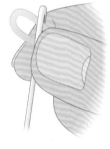

5 With your other hand, push the eye of the needle down between your tightly pinched finger and thumb and at the same time easing the loop through the eye.

6 Push the needle up the strand of yarn until it is off the loop and threaded onto a single strand of the yarn.

How to sew in yarn ends
Weave ends in and out of the work over approximately 2 in. (5 cm) on the wrong side of the crochet, keeping to the same area of color in the design.

Reading a pattern

Reading a pattern commonly puts people off crochet, but it shouldn't! In this book, we have set out the patterns in a format that is easy to understand. The abbreviations are simple and self explanatory. Where we have Special Abbreviations, we have fully explained how to do these stitches in each Workshop.

Crochet pattern instructions will start with a title followed by a brief introduction with a little detail about the project. The patterns in this book then continue with various sections in this order:

Measurements

The measurement of the crochet project will be given in inches and centimeters. This is the size of the finished project.

Materials section

This will give you a list of all the things you need to make the project.

Type of yarn: The brand name and type of the yarn that has been used in the project appears first. This is just a guide and other brands can be used providing you use a yarn of the same thickness and type, and the gauge works out the same (see Gauge on page 22).

Amount of balls/hanks required: Your pattern indicates approximately how many balls (or hanks) of yarn you will need. Typically yarn balls (and hanks) weigh 1¾oz (50g) or 3½oz (100g) each. Some specialty yarns, such as mohair, are sold in ⅞oz (25g) balls because mohair is a very light yarn. The length required of each yarn is often given in the pattern as well. If you decide to use a different brand, it's essential that you buy the same length as the yarn listed because a different yarn may contain less yarn in each ball.

Yarn colors: If several colors are used, these are usually given a letter reference, such as A, B, C or D, which will be referred to in the row-by-row section of the pattern. If the project has a main color, this will be referred to as MC.

Crochet hook size: US and metric hook sizes are provided in the instructions. These are recommended sizes to be used for this project and are based on the gauge given (see Gauge on page 22). They are a guide only and crochet hook sizes can vary depending on your gauge.

Extra materials: Sometimes you will need additional materials other than the usual yarn, crochet hook, and scissors for your project. For example, you'll need a pillow form for pillows. I always use feather pillow forms, although I'm allergic to feathers! I've used polyester-filled forms in the past, but they lose their shape. Feather ones last much longer and are only a little more expensive.

Ribbons are great to embellish crochet. Crochet is usually a loose and open fabric and ideal for threading ribbons through. Buttons are often needed for garments or for decoration. If you are using buttons for buttonholes, remember that yarn is stretchy so make sure buttons are big enough or they will get lost in the crochet fabric.

Beads can really enhance crochet. I find that beads work best on finer yarns and not on chunky ones. I use "seed" beads. They are shaped like little seeds with a hole in the center that is big enough for yarn. When buying beads, check with the supplier that the holes are big enough for the yarn you're using to go through.

Sometimes it helps if you can line crochet, for example in a bag or a purse. If you can line the item with fabric, this will control the stretchiness of the crochet. I always line the handles of my bags too, otherwise you are very limited on how much you can put in the bag. You don't need to know how to use a sewing machine, you can easily hand stitch linings into place.

Standard crochet abbreviations

These abbreviations are short forms to explain stitches. Please use this list as a reference, but once you start reading patterns, these will become obvious to you. Special abbreviations appear with the individual patterns.

alt	alternate
approx.	approximately
beg	begin(ning)
CC	contrasting color
ch	chain
cm	centimeter(s)
cont	continu(e)(ing)
dc	double crochet
dec	decrease
dtr	double treble
g	gram(s)
hdc	half double
in	inch(es)
inc	increase
lp(s)	loop(s)
m	meter(s)
mm	millimeter(s)
MC	main color
oz	ounce(s)
patt(s)	pattern(s)
rep	repeat
RS	right side
sc	single crochet
sp(s)	space(s)
ss	slip stitch
st(s)	stitch(es)
tch	turning chain
tog	together
tr	treble
trtr	triple treble
WS	wrong side
yd	yard(s)
yoh	yarn over hook

Gauge

The gauge for this project is given using the hook size, yarn and stitch listed. (See Gauge on page 22 for more details.)

Instructions for making the crochet pieces

This is an exact guide on how to make each of the pieces needed for the project—row by row. This needs to be followed stitch by stitch and line by line. It's essential to use a marker on your pattern to denote where you are in the instruction. The instructions will guide you through each step and should be followed in order.

You will usually find stitch counts at the end of rows and rounds and these are shown in brackets. A good designer will put these into the patterns as it really helps if you count the stitches at the end of each row or round, particularly if you are a beginner or not yet confident. If you have the incorrect amount of stitches, it will completely throw out your stitch count for the next and subsequent rows/rounds.

Understanding standard brackets, square brackets, and asterisks

A pattern can sometimes look daunting with so many brackets and asterisks all over it, but they are there to help you understand the pattern. As a rule, standard brackets are there to give you additional information and square brackets mean either a repeat or to show a group of stitches.

Square brackets: These are often used to group stitches together that are worked into the same place, for example "*3ch, [2dc, 2ch, 3dc] in same corner sp.*" They are also used for repeats—"*[4ch, 1sc in next ch sp] twice.*" This means that you repeat only the instruction inside the brackets once more before continuing with the rest of the pattern.

Standard brackets: As a rule, standard brackets are there to give you additional information about the instruction, for example "*4ch (counts as 1tr)."*

Asterisks: You will often find asterisks (* and **) in the pattern. These will show the beginning (and also sometimes the end) of sections of pattern that are repeated and there could be square brackets inside these asterisks that show stitch groups or repeated stitch sequences.

Finishing instructions

In the finishing instructions of a pattern you'll find guidance on how to put a garment together, how to add any embellishments, or occasionally how to press.

Charts

Many patterns include a symbol chart. I used to stay away from these because I thought they looked too complicated, but now I can't do without them—they are not as confusing as they first appear. The symbols relate to the height of the stitches. A chain is represented by a little oval shape which looks like a chain stitch, a single crochet by a little cross, and then the symbols increase in height in relation to the height of the stitches. It's really useful to use symbol charts to see exactly where a stitch should go on the row or round. You will also find patterns written slightly differently by different designers and from different countries. For example, there are many interesting patterns from Japan at the moment, and if you can read a symbol chart, you won't need to learn Japanese first. Also US and UK stitches have different terminology (see page 155), but the chart symbols are universal.

The symbols for each stitch are given next to the stitch in the step-by-step instructions, but they are also gathered here so you can find them quickly.

Symbol charts

We have included many crochet symbol diagrams in this book. These are universal symbols and are a really useful guide to visually see where to put the stitches. Where the symbol points to a chain or chain space, it means you have to make the stitch into the chain space and not directly into the loop of the chain. The following are basic symbols. Any special symbols are given with the individual charts.

O   **ch** chain

·   **ss** slip stitch

+   **sc** single crochet

T   **hdc** half double crochet

ꓕ   **dc** double crochet

ꓕ   **tr** treble

ꓕ   **dtr** double treble

ꓕ   **trtr** triple treble

▶   starting pointer

◁   ending pointer

Blocking, steaming, and pressing

Blocking means pinning out your work to achieve a neat and even shape.
I never used to block my pieces and, eager to get my work finished,
would sew it up without blocking, steaming, or pressing. Now that has
all changed and I always block and steam. It makes a huge difference,
by flattening out and getting rid of any creases or curls at the edges.

Whether you steam or press your work will depend on the yarn fiber you are using and you should always check the yarn label first for any special care instructions. Mohair and some acrylics shouldn't be blocked at all. If you are not sure try blocking the gauge swatch first.

Block your work on a flat, padded surface such as an ironing board. Some people make their own blocking boards or you can buy them commercially. I have found an ironing board works for most projects and if the project is too big then I will place a pile of towels on the table and use those—or just use the carpeted floor.

Always use a tape measure when pinning out your projects and stretch or ease your work gently to achieve the right measurement.

If you're steaming your work, large glass or plastic-headed pins work best, if pressing use pins that don't have plastic ends, or they may melt under the iron.

Steaming
First block out your work, generally with the wrong side facing. Using the steamer setting on the iron and pushing the steaming button, release the vapor and hold the iron approximately 1 in. (2.5 cm) above the work, but not touching it. This will dampen the work. Allow it to dry naturally and if possible leave blocked overnight.

Pressing
First block out your work with the wrong side facing upward. Do not press directly onto the yarn. Use a damp cotton cloth placed over the top of the work and then gently place the iron onto the damp cloth, just dabbing it lightly. Pressing tends to flatten the fibers of the yarn and steaming is preferable.

Cold blocking
If using acrylics or mohair try cold blocking, in which you shape your project on the board and pin it in place. Cover the item with dampened bath towels and leave to dry naturally.

Caring for your crochet
After you've made something beautiful, it's important to take care of it. Crochet is often a "holey" fabric and so it's easy to catch your fingers or toes in it and stretch it. Take care of your crochet, don't leave it in direct sunlight or it will fade, and keep blankets folded when not in use.

As far as washing instructions go, you must follow the washing instructions on the ball band. If your yarn is 100% wool, then it's always better to play safe and hand wash it. I recently made a sweater as a sample for this book (see page 72) and very foolishly and without thinking put it in the washing machine and—although it was on a cool wash—it shrank and I'm now on a diet so I can fit into it! It's not worth all your long hours of work and pleasure going to waste due to a moment of time cutting.

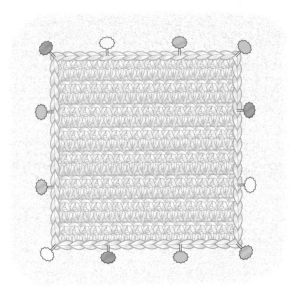

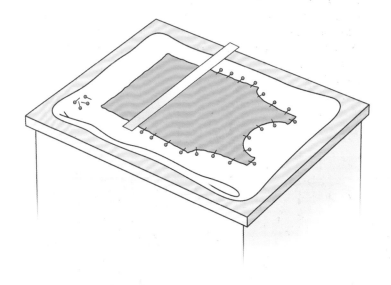

Section 2
Workshops and Projects

Workshop 1

The Basics

Learning to crochet with straight edges is vital. It is important to always go into the first stitch and the last stitch to avoid unintentionally making a decrease and creating a triangular shape at the end of the row. You'll also sometimes be instructed to go into one of the turning chains from the previous row. It's also important to be able to recognize the right and wrong side of the work. In addition this Workshop covers a basic edging, which you will use to embellish your first project—a Cotton Placemat.

Crocheting in the first stitch and last stitch

At the beginning or end of each straight row you will be instructed in the pattern to make a turning chain (tch), which will take your stitch up to the right height of the work (see Turning Chains on page 18).

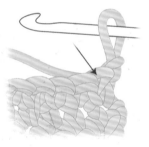

Working into the first stitch of a single crochet row.

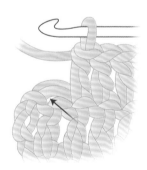

Working into the last stitch of a single crochet row.

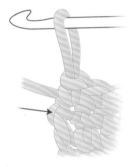

Working the last stitch into the turning chain of a single crochet row.

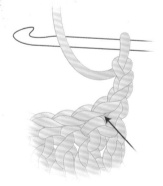

Working into the first stitch of a double crochet row.

Working into the last stitch of a double crochet row.

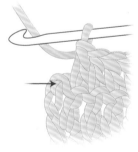

Working the last stitch into the turning chain of a double crochet row.

Right side and wrong side

Generally the right side of the work is smoother and the stitches flatter, while the wrong side has a more knobbly texture. However, it's sometimes difficult to see the difference, especially with single crochet, because the individual stitches are small and harder to see.

I usually check my right side by looking at the foundation row and first row of my stitches. The foundation chains have a linked rope effect and stand out more on the right side.

Single crochet right side.

Single crochet wrong side.

Half double crochet right side.

Half double crochet wrong side.

Double crochet right side.

Double crochet wrong side.

Single crochet edging

A single crochet edging is the base for most decorative edgings and neatens up the sides of crochet really well. It can also be used to make a frame in a contrasting color to create a good effect.

A single crochet edging usually starts at a corner and you will be instructed in the pattern where to join the yarn. There are usually 2 or 3 stitches made in the corner to create the corner shape, then you will be instructed to make single crochet stitches along the edge to the next corner, and so on until you have worked single crochet around the whole piece. A single crochet edging is usually worked on the right side of the work.

When you are working along the sides it's not always obvious where to place your hook or how to place the stitches evenly. I use either pin or stitch markers, placing them at the halfway and quarter points, then I divide the number of stitches required along the edge into four so that as I get to each marker I know I have placed the stitches evenly.

Joining with slip stitch

The edging is worked around the entire placemat, so for a neat finish you will have to join the end to the beginning with a slip stitch. This same technique is used whenever you need to join the last stitch to the first when making rounds and you will be instructed in the pattern where to place the hook.

1 Work the single crochet edging all around. After completing the last stitch, insert the hook into the top of the first stitch and wrap the yarn over the hook.

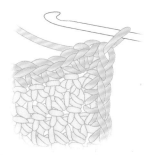

2 Pull the yarn through both the stitch and loop on the hook to join the two stitches (1 loop on hook). Fasten off the yarn as explained in Getting Started, Fastening off, page 23.

Cotton Placemats

This is a great first project. You'll learn how to crochet in straight lines in a very basic single crochet stitch. Mix and match the colors and the edging to suit your color scheme. These are made using cotton, so are easy for washing!

techniques used

Stitches—single crochet

Making a simple rectangle of crochet

Adding a 2-round single crochet edging around a rectangle

Joining rounds with a slip stitch

placemat measurements

Finished placemat measures 12 x 9¼ in. (30.5 x 23.5 cm), including edging.

yarns

Rowan *Cotton Glacé* (100% cotton) lightweight (light worsted) yarn

For six placemats
2 x 1¾ oz (50g) balls—approx. 250yd (230m)—of each of six colors:

A 724 Bubbles (pink)
B 849 Winsor (teal blue)
C 749 Sky (pale blue)
D 833 Ochre (yellow)
E 725 Ecru (off-white)
F 841 Garnet (dark purple)

hook

US size E-4 (3.5 mm) crochet hook

gauge

19 sts x 24 rows over a 4 in. (10 cm) square worked in single crochet using a US size E-4 (3.5 mm) hook.

abbreviations

ch	chain
rep	repeat
RS	right side
sc	single crochet
ss	slip stitch
st(s)	stitch(es)
WS	wrong side

The colorways

The six placemats are each worked in a different color, with a contrasting edging as follows:
Colorway 1: Placemat in A, edging in B
Colorway 2: Placemat in B, edging in A
Colorway 3: Placemat in C, edging in A
Colorway 4: Placemat in D, edging in C
Colorway 5: Placemat in E, edging in D
Colorway 6: Placemat in F, edging in E

To make the placemats

(Make one each in A, B, C, D, E, and F)
Foundation chain: Make 55ch.
Row 1 (RS): 1sc in 2nd ch from hook, 1sc in each ch to end. *54 sc.*
Row 2: 1ch, 1sc in each sc to end.
(Mark the right side of the work with a colored thread, so you will know which side to end on.)
Rep Row 2 until work measures 8½ in. (21.5 cm), ending on a WS row.
Cut off yarn, but do not fasten off.

To work the single-crochet edging

With the loop still on the hook after the last row and with the RS facing, work a single crochet edging in rounds using a contrasting color.
Round 1 (RS):
Along top of placemat—Using contrasting edging color, 1ch to draw new color through loop on hook, 3sc in first sc (corner st of placemat). Continue along top edge, making 1sc in each sc along top of placemat to last sc (next corner st), 3sc in corner st.
Along first side edge—*Measure halfway down first side edge and mark with either a stitch or pin marker, 17sc evenly along side edge to marker, 17sc to next corner st.**
Along bottom of placemat—3sc in corner st, 52sc evenly along bottom edge to next corner (working 1sc in each ch along underside of foundation chain).
Along second side edge—3sc in corner st; rep from * to ** as for first side edge. Join round with a ss in first sc.
Do not turn the work, but continue with RS facing.
Round 2 (RS): 1ch, 1sc in first sc, 2sc in next sc (corner st), 1sc in each sc to next corner st (sc at center of 3-sc group), *2sc in center st of corner, 1sc in each sc to next corner st; rep from * to end, join with a ss in first sc.
Fasten off.

To finish the placemats

Using a yarn sewing needle, sew in all yarn ends.
Block and press on the wrong side with a damp cloth.

Workshop 2

Making a Traditional Square

Squares are very popular in crochet and there are hundreds of different designs. They often start as a circle and the traditional (granny) square is a great way to begin. In this Workshop we're going to show you how to make a chain ring (circle), how to make stitches into a ring and how to join a round with a slip stitch. We also cover joining squares and making double groups, as well as looking at chain spaces and how to count stitches. The project, Squares Baby Blanket, puts all this into practice.

Making a ring (circle)

When making a chain ring you usually start with 4–6 chains, depending on how much space you need inside the ring to make the stitches in the first round.

1 Make a slip knot and then the number of chains instructed in the pattern, insert the crochet hook into the first chain that you made (not into the slip knot), yarn over hook, then pull the yarn through the chain and through the loop on your hook at the same time, creating a slip stitch and forming a ring.

2 You will now have a circle ready to proceed with your pattern.

3 After making the ring you'll be instructed to make a number of chains to bring your work up to the right height for the first stitch of the first round. For the project in this Workshop we are working with doubles so for this stitch we need to make 3 chains.

Making stitches into a ring

Keep an eye on where the center of the ring is. I usually stick my finger into the hole to define it—this can be neatened up later when sewing in ends.

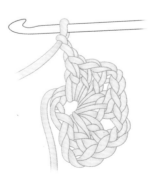

As you are making the stitches and chains to create this first round you may feel that you are running out of space in the ring. If so ease the stitches round so they are more bunched up, which will give you more space in the ring, and take care not to make your new stitches over the top of the first stitches or chains made in this round.

Enclosing a yarn tail

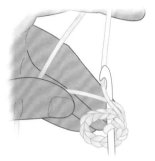

You may find that the yarn tail gets in the way; you can enclose this into the stitches as you go by placing the tail at the back as you wrap the yarn. This also saves having to sew this tail end in later.

Counting stitches

Checking your work regularly is vital so you will need to be able to see how many stitches you have made.

Chain stitches

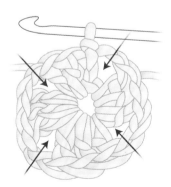

Chain spaces are the gaps created by making chains between the double groups.

Joining a round with a slip stitch

Most rounds are joined with a slip stitch in the top of the first chains or stitches in the round, unless you are working in a spiral (see Workshop 6, page 62). For the project in this Workshop we start with 3 chains, so count the first 3 chains from the bottom upward and then place the hook in the third chain and make the slip stitch. This will now complete the circle.

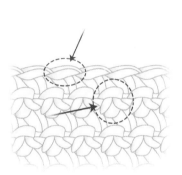

1 Single crochet stitches have short "stalks" so it's sometimes easier to count the Vs at the top of the stitches.

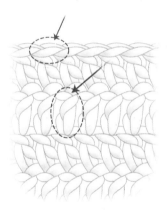

2 There are two ways to check the number of doubles you've made. A double is taller than a single crochet so it is easily checked by counting the "stalks," but you can also count the Vs at the top of the stitches as for single crochet.

You can make stitches or groups of stitches into a chain space instead of into the top of a stitch. The example shows three double stitches made into a chain space between two groups of three doubles in the previous row/round.

> **TIP**
> At the end of a round check you have the right number of stitches and chain spaces before continuing to the next round.

Creating a square

A square is created by making stitches and chain spaces into the same space or stitches, which makes a fan shape and creates the corner. This is the basis of all corners on crochet square motifs, although some use different stitches and patterns.

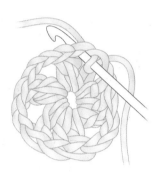   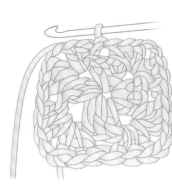

1 Slip stitch across the next two stitches as instructed in the pattern—the slip stitches don't create height, they just take the yarn across the stitches toward the chain space, where the pattern for the next round will start.

2 To make the slip stitches, insert the hook into each of the next two stitches, picking up both loops of each stitch (see Getting Started: Slip Stitch, page 19). Now, slip stitch into the chain space.

3 To make a corner from a circle, you need to make a group of stitches into the same chain space.

4 If you continue with the pattern you will create four corners and will have made a square from a circle.

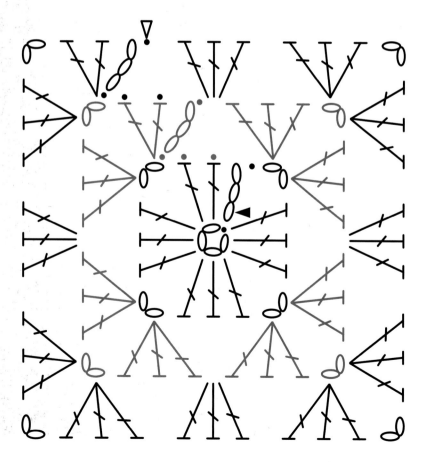

Square motif chart

key		
⬭	**ch**	chain
•	**ss**	slip stitch
⊤	**dc**	double crochet
▶		starting pointer
◁		ending pointer

Joining squares: Overcast method

There are several methods of joining—which joining technique is best will depend on the project. In the Baby Blanket project in this Workshop I have used an overcast join, which gives a nice flat seam and is the most simple and common joining technique.

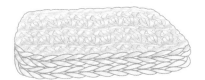

1 Thread a yarn sewing needle with the yarn you're using in the project. Don't cut it too long because this will make it hard to pull through and the yarn is likely to get twisted as you're sewing. Generally speaking, the yarn should be about the length of your arm. Match up two squares with the right sides together.

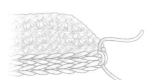

2 Insert the needle in one corner in the top loops of the stitches of both squares and pull up the yarn, leaving a tail of about 2 in. (5 cm). Go into the same place with the needle and pull up the yarn again; repeat two or three times to secure the yarn at the start of the seam.

3 Join the squares together by picking up the loops at the top of the stitches of corresponding squares across the top to the end. Continue in this way, by picking up another two squares and continuing to do the overcast stitch until all the squares are joined in the row of squares.

TIPS
• If you're using a particularly chunky or bobbly yarn in a project, choose a finer yarn in the same color to use for joining.
• If you're making a multi color item, use one of the paler colors—I used the pale blue to join the squares in my blanket because there was more of this left over from the project.

Edging: Double groups

This is a very effective and simple edging that works well with the traditional Squares Baby Blanket project in this Workshop (see opposite). A double group edging is created by making three doubles in the same space each time all around the blanket. The instructions in the pattern will guide you where to place the doubles and where to place the double two stitches together (decrease). The double two together decrease over the joins avoids the edging having too many stitches—which would make it curl—and creates a nice straight edge.

Double two stitches together (dc2tog)

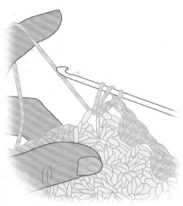

1 Yarn over hook, insert the hook into the next space, yarn over hook, pull the yarn through the work (3 loops on hook).

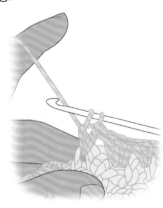

2 Yarn over hook, pull the yarn through two loops on the hook (2 loops on hook).

3 Yarn over hook, insert the hook into the next space (in the next square).

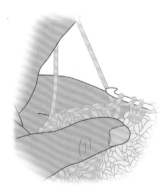

4 Yarn over hook, pull the yarn through the work (4 loops on hook).

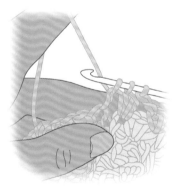

5 Yarn over hook, pull the yarn through 2 loops on the hook (3 loops on hook).

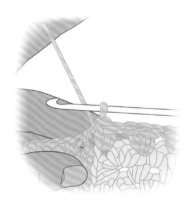

6 Yarn over hook, pull the yarn through all 3 loops on the hook (1 loop on hook). One double two stitches together (decrease) made.

double two stitches together (dc2tog) in symbols

Squares Baby Blanket

This blanket is made using traditional "granny" squares. They are the simplest squares to make, and this project is perfect for practicing doubles, creating squares, making a simple edging and using a double decrease. A great project for those starting out, the blanket will be a much appreciated gift for a baby.

techniques used

Stitches—double crochet

Joining rounds with a slip stitch

Making traditional crochet squares

Sewing together traditional squares using overcast stitch

Working a double-group edging

Crocheting 2 double crochet together (dc2tog decrease)

blanket measurements

Blanket is 11 squares wide x 13 squares long (a total of 143 squares).

Finished blanket measures 28¾ x 33¾ in. (74.5 x 87.5 cm), including edging, which is ⅝ in. (1.5 cm) wide.

yarns

Debbie Bliss Baby Cashmerino (55% merino wool, 33% microfiber, 12% cashmere) lightweight (sport-weight) yarn

2 x 1¾ oz (50g) balls—approx. 274yd (250m)—each of two colors:

A 202 Light Blue (pale blue)
B 034 Red

1 x 1¾ oz (50g) ball—approx. 137yd (125m)—each of seven colors:

C 071 Pool (medium blue)
D 601 Baby Pink (pale pink)
E 101 Ecru (off-white)
F 078 Lipstick (bright pink)
G 066 Amber (mustard yellow)
H 002 Apple (light green)
J 010 Lilac

hook

US size E-4 (3.5 mm) crochet hook

gauge

Each square measures 2½ x 2½ in. (6.5 x 6.5 cm) using a US size E-4 (3.5 mm) hook.

abbreviations

ch	chain
cont	continu(e)(ing)
dc	double crochet
rep	repeat
RS	right side
sp(s)	space(s)
ss	slip stitch
st(s)	stitch(es)
tog	together
yoh	yarn over hook

special abbreviation

dc2tog (double crochet 2 together) over 2 ch sps: Yoh and insert hook in next sp, yoh and pull yarn through work (3 loops on hook), yoh and pull yarn through first 2 loops on hook (2 loops on hook), yoh and insert hook in next sp (on next square), yoh and pull yarn through work (4 loops on hook), yoh and pull yarn through first 2 loops on hook (3 loops on hook), yoh and pull yarn through all 3 loops on hook to complete the dc2tog.

Square motif chart

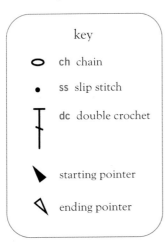

key

○ ch chain

• ss slip stitch

T dc double crochet

▶ starting pointer

▽ ending pointer

TIP
Sew in the yarn ends after completing each square, using a yarn sewing needle.

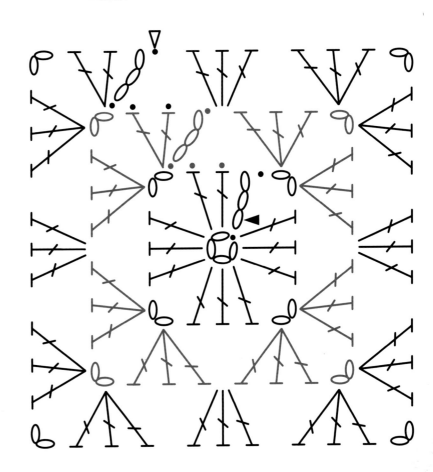

To make the squares
Work each square as follows:

Foundation ring: Make 4ch and join with a ss in first ch to form a ring.

Round 1 (RS): 3ch (counts as first dc), 2dc in ring, 2ch, [3dc in ring, 2ch] 3 times, join with a ss in top of first 3-ch. *Four 3-dc groups.*

Cont in rounds with RS always facing you.

Round 2: 1ss in each of next 2dc, 1ss in next 2-ch sp, 3ch (counts as first dc), [2dc, 2ch, 3dc] in same ch sp (corner), *[3dc, 2ch, 3dc] in next 2-ch sp; rep from * twice more, join with a ss in top of first 3-ch.

Round 3: 1ss in each of next 2dc, 1ss in next 2-ch sp, 3ch (counts as first dc), [2dc, 2ch, 3dc] in same 2-ch sp (corner), 3dc in next sp between next two 3-dc groups, *[3dc, 2ch, 3dc] in next 2-ch sp (corner), 3dc in next sp between next two 3-dc groups; rep from * twice more, join with a ss in top of first 3-ch.
Fasten off.

To join the squares
Using a yarn sewing needle, sew in any remaining yarn ends. Block and press each square on the wrong side. With right sides facing up, place the squares on a flat surface and arrange them in 13 horizontal rows (length) of 11 squares each (width). Make sure the colored squares are evenly spaced.

With right sides together and using A (pale blue) and a yarn sewing needle, join the squares in 13 rows using overcast stitch. Then join the rows together.
Block and lightly press the seams on the wrong side of the blanket.

To work the treble-group edging
Round 1 (RS): With RS facing and using A (pale blue), join yarn with a ss in a 2-ch sp at one corner of the blanket, 3ch (counts as first dc), [2dc, 2ch, 3dc] in same corner sp, 3dc in each of next 2 sps between 3-dc groups, *1dc in last sp of this square (corner of square), dc2tog over same corner sp and first corner sp of next square (see Special Abbreviation), 1dc in same corner sp, 3dc in each of next 2 sps between 3-dc groups*; rep from * to * to next blanket corner, **[3dc, 2ch, 3dc] in corner 2-ch sp, rep from * to * to next blanket corner; rep from ** to end, join with a ss in top of first 3-ch.

Round 2: 1ss in each of next 2dc, 1ss in corner 2-ch sp, 3ch (counts as 1dc), [2dc, 2ch, 3dc] in same corner sp, 3dc in next and each sp between dc groups to next corner (skip each dc2tog in previous round, do not make doubles in center of these dc2tog), *[3dc, 2ch, 3dc] in corner 2-ch sp, 3dc in next and each sp between dc groups to next corner; rep from * to end, join with a ss in first 3-ch.
Fasten off.

Workshop 3

Crocheting in the Round

In this Workshop we look at working in the round to create a circular piece of fabric, which is put into practice with the project in which we make a Round Pillow cover. We also cover a different method of joining, by working a single crochet seam. Embellishments covered in this section are a shell edging, five-petal flower, leaves, and French knots.

Working in the round

To crochet in the round you always have to start with a small ring (circle). When crocheting in circles the sequences of stitches are called rounds—if you see "round" in the pattern, you'll know that this will be a circular pattern, while rows are worked backward and forward to create a piece of fabric with straight edges.

There are two ways to create a circular piece of crocheted fabric, in this Workshop you will join each circle with a slip stitch. The other way to make a circle is using a spiral technique, which is covered in Workshop 6 on page 62. Both circles start from the smallest point and use increases to expand the round shape.

To start the circle make a ring as directed in Workshop 2, Making a ring (circle) on page 34. In the first round make 3ch (to bring your work up to the right height—you will be working with doubles in this project). This first 3ch counts as the first double. Make the following 11dc all into the ring. It's vital to move the stitches around the ring just made to make space for all 11 doubles (see Workshop 2, Making stitches into a ring, second diagram, on page 34) and finish the round as instructed. The next rounds are increases.

1 Double crochet in the same place as the last slip stitch.

2 The next stitch is the one directly next to the stitch into which you've just made a double crochet. Make sure you pick up both loops of this stitch. 2dc into the same st— making two double crochet into the same stitch creates an increase.

Before starting on each round of the Workshop pattern, make sure you count each stitch in the round just worked and then make the slip stitch to join the round. It's really useful from this point to follow the chart—this enables you to see exactly where the stitches go and also to see clearly how the circle gradually increases.

Single crochet seam

With a single crochet seam you join two pieces together using a crochet hook and working a single crochet stitch through both pieces, instead of sewing them together with a tail of yarn and a yarn sewing needle. This makes a quick and strong seam and gives a slightly raised finish to the edging. On the Round Pillow cover project in this Workshop I have used a single crochet seam working on the right side, which gives a clear line to place the shell stitch edging around the outside of the cover.

1 Start by lining up the two pieces with wrong sides together. Insert the hook in the top two loops of the stitch of the first piece, then into the corresponding stitch on the second piece.

2 Complete the single crochet stitch as normal and continue on next stitches as directed in the pattern. This gives a raised effect if the single crochet stitches are made on the right side of the work.

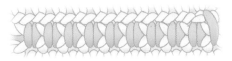

3 You can work with the wrong side of the work facing (with the pieces right side facing) if you don't want this effect and it still creates a good strong join.

Shell edging

A shell edging is really pretty and is easy once you have mastered double crochet and making doubles into the same stitch. This pattern is made up of 5 double crochet made in one stitch to create a "fan" or "shell" effect. Try out this sample before you add the edging to your project.

Make 23ch.
Row 1 (RS): 1dc in 4th ch from hook, 1dc in each ch to end.
Row 2 (WS): 3ch, 1dc in each st to end.

Row 3 (RS): 1ch, ss in first st, *skip next st, 5dc in next st, skip next st, ss in next st; rep from * to end, ss in top of first 3ch. Fasten off.

Shell edging chart

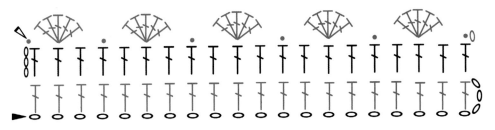

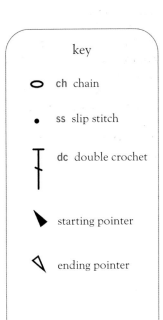

key

○ ch chain

• ss slip stitch

⊤ dc double crochet

▶ starting pointer

▽ ending pointer

5-petal flower

This flower is the perfect introduction to making flowers. It uses all the stitches and techniques that you have learned in this Workshop and makes a very effective embellishment.

Foundation ring: Using a US size G-6 (4 mm) hook, make 6ch and join with a ss in first ch to form a ring.

Round 1 (RS): 1ch, 15sc in ring, join with a ss in first sc.
Cont in rounds with RS facing.

Round 2: *3ch, 1dc in each of next 2sc, 3ch, 1ss in next sc; rep from * 4 times more. *5 petals.*
Fasten off.

Using a yarn sewing needle, sew in the beginning yarn tail around center to close hole. Sew in the other yarn end on the wrong side of the flower. Using a yarn sewing needle and a contrasting color, embroider three French knots in the center of each flower.

5-petal flower chart

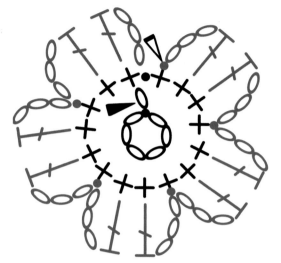

key		
O	**ch**	chain
•	**ss**	slip stitch
+	**sc**	single crochet
T	**dc**	double crochet
▶		starting pointer
◁		ending pointer

French knots

French knots make little beads of yarn on the surface of the work.

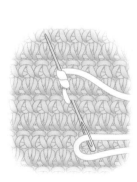

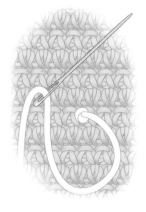

1 Thread the yarn into a yarn sewing needle. Bring the yarn out at your starting point from the back of the work to the front and where you want the French knot to sit, leaving a tail of yarn at the back that you will sew in later. Pick up a couple of strands across the stitch on the front of the work close to the place the yarn has been pulled through.

2 Wrap the yarn around the needle two or three times, pushing the wraps close to the crochet piece.

3 Take the needle in one hand and pull it through the wraps, holding the wraps in place near the crochet piece with the other hand. This will form a little knot close to the crochet piece.

4 Insert the needle (from the right side) very close to the knot and push the needle through to the wrong side (French knot made).

Leaves

These leaves are made by making stitches into the foundation chain (see Getting started, Foundation chain, page 18), then working into the underside of the same foundation chain.

Foundation chain: Using a US size G-6 (4 mm) hook and G, make 8ch.

Round 1 (RS): 1sc in 2nd ch from hook, 1hdc in next ch, 1dc in each of next 2 ch, 2dc in next ch, 1hdc in next ch, 1sc in next ch (this is the last ch), 2ch, with RS of work still facing, turn work so that the underside of the foundation chain is uppermost and continue working around the other side of this chain, 1sc in first ch, 1hdc in next ch, 2dc in next ch, 1dc in each of next 2 ch, 1hdc in next ch, 1sc in last ch, join with a ss in first sc of round (in tip of leaf). Fasten off.

Leaf chart

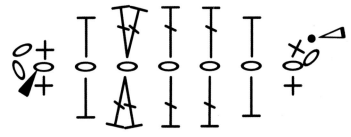

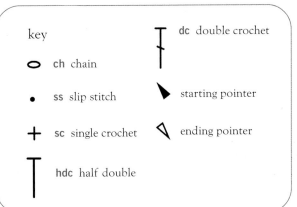

key

○ **ch** chain	**T** **dc** double crochet
• **ss** slip stitch	**▶** starting pointer
+ **sc** single crochet	**▷** ending pointer
T **hdc** half double	

Round Pillow

Crocheting in the round is one of the pleasures and advantages of crochet. This is a gorgeous pillow cover, very pretty and perfect for practicing doubles. The yarn used in this project is a super chunky, very soft yarn and crochets up really quickly, too. The flowers and leaves are a charming embellishment, but you could use any of the other flowers in this book instead if you prefer.

techniques used

Stitches—double crochet, single crochet, half double crochet

Making a crochet circle

Joining rounds with a slip stitch

Increasing with doubles

Making a five-petal flower

Crocheting a leaf

Embroidering French knots

Working a single-crochet seam

Adding a shell edging

pillow cover measurements

Finished pillow cover fits a pillow form 16 in. (40 cm) in diameter.

yarns

pillow cover:
Debbie Bliss *Paloma* (60% alpaca, 40% wool) super-bulky-(super-chunky-) weight yarn

4 x 1¾ oz (50g) hanks—approx. 284yd (260m)—of main color:

MC 28 Jade (turquoise)

flowers:
Scraps of light worsted (DK) weight yarn in six contrasting colors:

A off-white
B pale orange
C orange
D pink
E light pink
F red

leaves:
Scraps of light worsted (DK) weight yarn in one color:

G pale green

hooks

US size K-10½ (7 mm) crochet hook
US size G-6 (4 mm) crochet hook

extras

16 in. (40 cm) round pillow form

gauge

10 sts x 4½ rows over a 4 in. (10 cm) square worked in double crochet using a US size K-10½ (7 mm) hook and MC.

abbreviations

ch	chain
cont	continu(e)(ing)
dc	double crochet
hdc	half double
rep	repeat
RS	right side
sc	single crochet
ss	slip stitch
st(s)	stitch(es)
WS	wrong side

To make the pillow cover front

Foundation ring: Using a US size K-10½ (7 mm) hook and MC, make 6ch and join with ss in first ch to form a ring.

Round 1 (RS): 3ch (counts as first dc), 11dc in ring, join with a ss in top of first 3-ch. *12 sts.*

Cont in rounds with RS always facing you.

Round 2: 3ch, 1dc in same place as last ss, 2dc in next st and every st to end of round, join with a ss in top of first 3-ch. *24 sts.*

Round 3: 3ch, 1dc in same place as last ss, *1dc in next st, 2dc in each of next 2 sts; rep from * to last 2 sts, 1dc in next st, 2dc in last st, join with a ss in top of first 3-ch. *40 sts.*

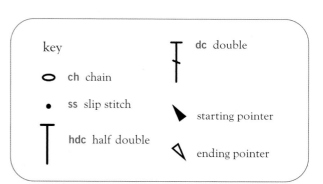

key

o **ch** chain

• **ss** slip stitch

hdc half double

dc double

▶ starting pointer

▷ ending pointer

Circles chart

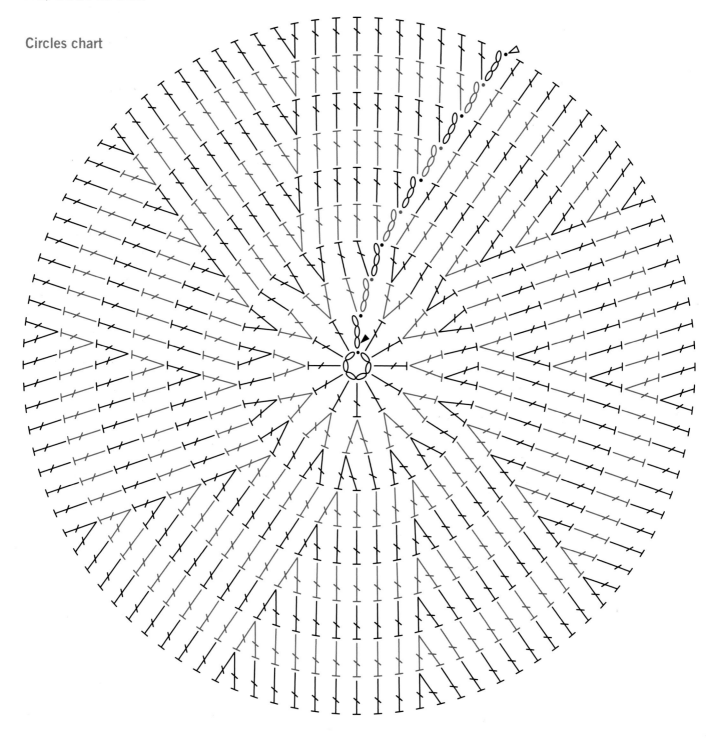

Round 4: 3ch, 1dc in same place as last ss, *1dc in each of next 3 sts, 2dc in next st; rep from * to last 3 sts, 1dc in each of last 3 sts, join with a ss in top of first 3-ch. *50 sts.*
Round 5: 3ch, 1dc in same place as last ss, *1dc in each of next 4 sts, 2dc in next st; rep from * to last 4 sts, 1dc in each of last 4 sts, join with a ss in top of first 3-ch. *60 sts.*
Round 6: 3ch, 1dc in same place as last ss, *1dc in each of next 5 sts, 2dc in next st; rep from *to last 5 sts, 1dc in each of last 5 sts, join with a ss in top of first 3-ch. *70 sts.*
Round 7: 3ch, 1dc in same place as last ss, *1dc in each of next 6 sts, 2dc in next st; rep from * to last 6 sts, 1dc in each of last 6 sts, join with a ss in top of first 3-ch. *80 sts.*
Round 8: 3ch, 1dc in same place as last ss, *1dc in each of next 7 sts, 2dc in next st; rep from * to last 7 sts, 1dc in each of last 7 sts, join with a ss in top of first 3-ch. *90 sts.*
Round 9: 3ch, 1dc in same place as last ss, *1dc in each of next 8 sts, 2dc in next st; rep from * to last 8 sts, 1dc in each of last 8 sts, join with a ss in top of first 3-ch. *100 sts.*
Fasten off.

To make the pillow cover back
Make exactly as for the front.

To make the five-petal flowers
(Make two in A, and one each in B, C, D, E and F)
Foundation ring: Using a US size G-6 (4 mm) hook, make 6ch and join with a ss in first ch to form a ring.
Round 1 (RS): 1ch, 15sc in ring, join with a ss in first dc.
Cont in rounds with RS facing.

5-petal flower chart

Leaf chart

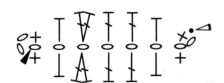

Round 2: *3ch, 1dc in each of next 2 sc, 3ch, 1ss in next dc; rep from * 4 times more. *5 petals.*
Fasten off.
Using a yarn sewing needle, sew in the beginning yarn tail around center to close hole. Sew in the other yarn end on the wrong side of the flower.
Using a yarn sewing needle and a contrasting color (A, B, C, D, E, F or G), embroider three French knots in the center of each flower.

To make the leaves
(Make six)
Foundation chain: Using a US size G-6 (4 mm) hook and G, make 8ch.
Round 1 (RS): 1sc in 2nd ch from hook, 1hdc in next ch, 1dc in each of next 2 ch, 2dc in next ch, 1hdc in next ch, 1sc in next ch (this is the last ch), 2ch, with RS of work still facing, turn work so that underside of foundation chain is uppermost and continue working around other side of this chain, 1sc in first ch, 1hdc in next ch, 2dc in next ch, 1dc in each of next 2 ch, 1hdc in next ch, 1sc in last ch, join with a ss in first sc of round (in tip of leaf).
Fasten off.

To finish the cover
Using a yarn sewing needle, sew in any yarn ends on the crochet pieces.
Place the pillow cover front on the pillow cover back, with wrong sides together, then join the layers with a single crochet seam as follows:
Using a US size K-10½ (7 mm) hook and MC, insert hook through a dc on both layers, yoh and draw a loop through, 1ch, then working through both layers with each st, work 1sc in same st as ss was worked, 1sc in each st until the opening is just big enough to push through the pillow form. Insert the pillow form. Cont in sc until the seam is complete (total of 100 sc around edge), then join with a ss in first sc. Do not cut off yarn.
To complete the pillow, work an edging all around the seam.

To work the shell edging
Round 1 (RS): Skip first sc, 5dc in next sc, skip next sc, 1ss in next sc, *skip next sc, 5dc in next sc, skip next sc, 1ss in next st; rep from * to end, working last ss in same place as ss at beginning of round. *25 shells made.*
Fasten off.

To sew on the flowers and leaves
Arrange the flowers and leaves at the center of the pillow cover front, so they are sitting within the first 3 or 4 rounds. Position one flower at the very center and the six remaining flowers around it. Position the ends of the leaves between the flowers so that they point outward. Sew the arrangement in place with a yarn sewing needle and matching yarn.

Workshop 4

Stripes and waves

Stripes can be used in a variety of ways, either in straight rows or to make wavy shapes such as in the wave and chevron stitch. This Workshop covers joining in a new yarn with double crochet, decreasing three doubles into one, and also explains how multiple stitches are indicated within patterns and how they can be adjusted to change the design. The project to try out all these new techniques is a pretty Wave and Chevron Stitch Scarf.

Using stripes

Stripes are made simply by changing the yarn color on subsequent rows/rounds. You can either change color on each row for a narrow stripe, or to make a thicker stripe use the same color for more rows. Stripes can also be made on rounds or squares to make concentric circles of different colors.

Changing color

Colors should be changed at the end of each row if possible, not in the middle unless indicated in the pattern. Do not fasten off when changing color—cut the old yarn leaving a tail of about 6 in. (15 cm), draw through a loop of the new color and then start to crochet in the new color (see Getting Started, Joining in a new ball of yarn, page 23).

If the ends of the old and new colors start to become loose, tie them in a single knot to hold them in place until you sew in the ends at the end of the project. Do not tie a double knot. Always sew in the ends along the same color stitches.

Joining a new yarn using double crochet in the middle of a row

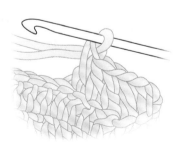 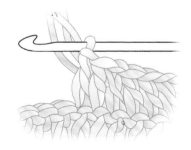

1 Make a double stitch as usual, but do not complete the stitch. When there are 2 loops remaining on the hook, drop the old yarn, catch the new yarn with the hook and pull it through these 2 loops.

2 Continue to crochet with the new yarn. Cut the strand of the old yarn about 6 in. (15 cm) from the crochet and leave it to drop at the back of the work so you can sew this end in later.

Working a decrease over three double crochet stitches (dc3tog)

This decrease takes three double crochet down into one stitch (a decrease). In the Wave & Chevron Stitch it is worked in conjunction with making three double crochet into one stitch (increase, see Getting Started, page 21).

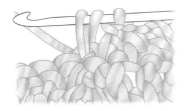

1 Yarn over hook, insert the hook in the next stitch (first of the three stitches), yarn over hook, pull the yarn through the work (3 loops on hook).

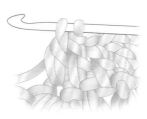

2 Yarn over hook, pull the yarn through the first two loops on the hook (2 loops on hook).

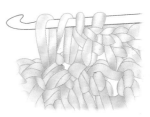

3 Yarn over hook, insert the hook in the next st (second of the three stitches), yarn over hook, pull the yarn through the work (4 loops on hook).

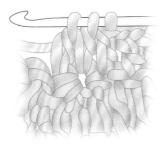

4 Yarn over hook, pull the yarn through the first two loops on the hook (3 loops on hook).

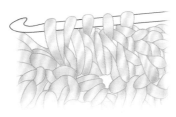

5 Yarn over hook, insert the hook in the next st (third of the three stitches), yarn over hook, pull the yarn through the work (now 5 loops on hook).

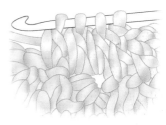

6 Yarn over hook, pull the yarn through the first two loops on the hook (4 loops on hook).

7 Yarn over hook, pull the yarn through all 4 loops on the hook (1 loop on hook).

double crochet three stitches together (dc3tog) in symbols

Wave and chevron stitch

There are many chevron crochet patterns but the Wave stitch I have used in the project with this Workshop is my favorite and a very popular stitch. It's the most asked-for stitch in all my Intermediate Crochet classes.

Multiples of 10 + 3 stitches.

Foundation chain: Using color A, make 33ch.
Row 1: 1dc in 3rd ch from hook, 1dc in each of next 3ch, dc3tog over next 3 ch, 1dc in each of next 3 ch, *3dc in next ch, 1dc in each of next 3 ch, dc3tog over next 3 ch, 1dc in each of next 3 ch; rep from * to last ch, 2dc in last ch.
Cut off yarn, but do not fasten off.
Row 2: Join next color, 3ch, 1dc in each of first 4 sts, dc3tog over next 3 sts, 1dc in each of next 3 sts, *3dc in next st, 1dc in each of next 3 sts, dc3tog over next 3 sts, 1dc in each of next 3 sts; rep from * to end, 2dc in top of 3-ch at end of row.
Rep Row 2, changing color on each row.

Wave and chevron stitch chart

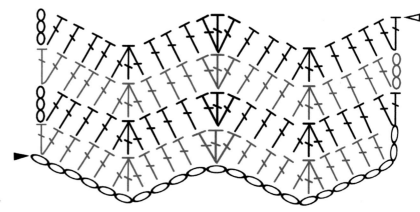

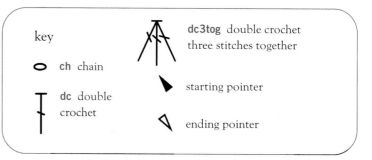

key

○ **ch** chain

┬ **dc** double crochet

▲ **dc3tog** double crochet three stitches together

▶ starting pointer

▷ ending pointer

1 The up curve is created by increasing stitches over the same increases from the previous rows, using double crochet.

2 The down curve is created by decreasing stitches over the same decreases from the previous rows. The pattern is the same for each row (repeat Row 2 each time) and you just follow it for the whole project, changing colors on each row.

Understanding multiples

Crochet reference stitch books often give you the repeat of the stitch in multiples; for this wave and chevron stitch "Multiples of 10 + 3," which means that a complete repeat takes 10 stitches, plus 3 stitches to allow for the turning chain.

If you would like to make a wider piece of crochet you need to work it out in multiples of the repeat: so for instance, 5 x 10 stitches = 50 stitches (for the pattern) plus an extra 3 stitches to allow for the turning chain on row 1.

If you want a narrower piece, make 20 stitches (2 repeats), plus add an extra 3 stitches for the turning chain.

Wave and Chevron Stitch Scarf

Stripes are great on scarves or blankets and combining them with Wave and Chevron stitch makes a very effective and interesting project. The stitch is one of my favorites —once you get the idea of the increases and decreases it's a very therapeutic stitch to use, and it's fun to experiment with the stripes. Don't be deterred by all the sewing in of ends—that can be therapeutic too!

The colorway
Work the scarf in a repeating stripe sequence of 1 row A, 1 row B, 1 row C, and 1 row D.

To make the scarf
Foundation chain: Using color A, make 33ch.
Row 1: 1dc in 3rd ch from hook, 1dc in each of next 3ch, dc3tog over next 3 ch, 1dc in each of next 3 ch, *3dc in next ch, 1dc in each of next 3 ch, dc3tog over next 3 ch, 1dc in each of next 3 ch; rep from * to last ch, 2dc in last ch.
Cut off yarn, but do not fasten off.
Row 2: Join next color, 3ch, 1dc in each of first 4 sts, dc3tog over next 3 sts, 1dc in each of next 3 sts, *3dc in next st, 1dc in each of next 3 sts, dc3tog over next 3 sts, 1dc in each of next 3 sts; rep from * to end, 2dc in top of 3-ch at end of row.
Rep Row 2 changing color on each row until work measures approximately 90 in. (228.5 cm) from beginning or until you run out of yarn, ending with color A.
Fasten off.

To finish the scarf
Using a yarn sewing needle, sew in all yarn ends.

---

techniques used

Stitches—double crochet

Working traditional wave and chevron stitch

Making decreases and increases in double crochet

Working with colors and stripes

scarf measurements

Finished scarf measures approximately 7½ in. (19 cm) wide x 90 in. (228.5 cm) long.

yarns

Debbie Bliss *Cashmerino Aran* (55% merino wool, 33% microfiber, 12% cashmere) worsted- (Aran-) weight yarn

2 x 1¾oz (50g) balls—approx. 197yd (180m)—of each of four colors:

A 042 Mulberry (purple)
B 027 Stone (beige)
C 061 Jade (blue-green)
D 603 Baby Pink (pale pink)

hook

US size H-8 (5 mm) crochet hook

gauge

15 sts x 9 rows over a 4 in. (10 cm) square worked in double crochet and using a US size H-8 (5 mm) hook.

abbreviations

ch	chain
dc	double crochet
rep	repeat
st(s)	stitch(es)
tog	together
yoh	yarn over hook

special abbreviation

dc3tog (double crochet 3 together decrease): Yoh, insert hook in next st, yoh, pull yarn through work (3 loops on hook), yoh, pull yarn through first 2 loops on hook (2 loops on hook), yoh, insert hook in next st, yoh, pull yarn through work (4 loops on hook), yoh, pull yarn through first 2 loops on hook (3 loops on hook), yoh, insert hook in next st, yoh, pull yarn through work (5 loops on hook) yoh, pull yarn through first 2 loops on hook (4 loops on hook), yoh, pull yarn through all 4 loops on hook (1 loop on hook).

Workshop 5

Clusters and Mattress Stitch Joining Seam

Clusters are groups of stitches joined together in the same stitch or over several stitches to create a textured or lacy effect. The pattern for this Workshop is for a Textured Pillow cover, which is made in straight rows so is an excellent way to practice these stitches without shaping. This section also covers the mattress stitch seam, which is an invisible method of joining two pieces of crochet, and making a large daisy chain flower.

Clusters

Clusters are groups of stitches, with each stitch only partly worked and then all joined at the end to form one stitch that creates a particular pattern and shape. They are most effective when made using a longer stitch such as double crochet.

Two-double crochet cluster (2dcCL)

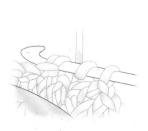

1 Yarn over hook, insert the hook in the stitch (or space).

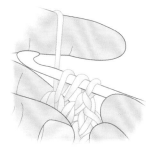

2 Yarn over hook, pull the yarn through the work (3 loops on hook).

3 Yarn over hook, pull the yarn through 2 loops on the hook (2 loops on hook).

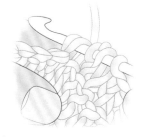

4 Yarn over hook, insert the hook in the same stitch (or space).

5 Yarn over hook, pull the yarn through the work (4 loops on hook).

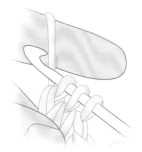

6 Yarn over hook, pull the yarn through 2 loops on the hook (3 loops on hook).

7 Yarn over hook, pull the yarn through all 3 loops on the hook (1 loop on hook). One two-double crochet cluster made.

two-double crochet cluster (2dcCL) in symbols

Texture pattern

This repeating texture pattern is used in the pillow for this Workshop.
Try it out first here.

Multiples of 10 + 4 stitches.

Foundation chain: Using a US size E-4 (3.5 mm) hook, make 24ch.

Row 1 (WS): 1dc in 4th ch from hook, *3ch, skip 2 ch, 1sc in next ch, 1ch, skip 1 ch, 1sc in next ch, 3ch, skip 2 ch, 1dc in next ch, 1ch, skip 1 ch, 1dc in next ch; rep from * to end.

Row 2 (RS): 1ch, 1sc in first dc, 1dc in first 1-ch sp (between first 2 dc), 2ch, *skip next 3-ch sp, [2dcCL, 1ch, 2dcCL, 1ch, 2dcCL] all in next 1-ch sp (between 2 sc), 2ch, skip next 3-ch sp**, 1sc in next 1-ch sp (between 2 dc), 2ch; rep from * ending last rep at **, skip last dc, 2sc in top of 3-ch at end of row.

Row 3 (WS): 1ch, 1sc in first sc, 1ch, skip next sc, 1sc in next 2-ch sp, *3ch, skip next 2dcCL, 1dc in next 1-ch sp (between 2dcCLs), 1ch, skip next 2dcCL, 1dc in next 1-ch sp (between 2dcCLs), 3ch, 1sc in next 2-ch sp, 1ch**, 1sc in next 2-ch sp; rep from * ending last rep at **, 1sc in last sc.

Row 4 (RS): 3ch, [2dcCL, 1ch, 2dcCL] all in first 1-ch sp (between 2 sc), 2ch, skip next 3-ch sp, 1sc in next 1-ch sp, (between 2 dc), 2ch, *skip next 3-ch sp, [2dcCL, 1ch, 2dcCL, 1ch, 2dcCL] all in next 1-ch sp (between 2 sc), 2ch, skip next 3-ch sp, 1sc in next 1-ch sp (between 2 dc), 2ch; rep from * to last 3-ch sp, skip last 3-ch sp, [2dcCL, 1ch, 2dcCL] all in next 1-ch sp (between last 2 sc), 1dc in last sc.

Row 5 (WS): 3ch, 1dc in first 1-ch sp (between 2dcCLs), 3ch, 1sc in next 2-ch sp, 1ch, 1sc in next 2-ch sp, *3ch, skip next 2dcCL, 1dc in next 1-ch sp (between 2dcCLs), 1ch, skip next 2dcCL, 1dc in next 1-ch sp (between 2dcCLs), 3ch, 1sc in next 2-ch sp, 1ch, 1sc in next 2-ch sp; rep from *, ending 3ch, skip next 2dcCL, 1dc in next 1-ch sp (between 2dcCLs), 1ch, 1dc in top of 3-ch at end of row.
Rep Rows 2–5 to form pattern.

Texture pattern chart

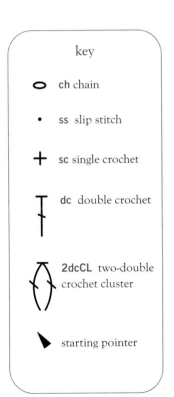

key

○ **ch** chain

• **ss** slip stitch

+ **sc** single crochet

T **dc** double crochet

⋀ **2dcCL** two-double crochet cluster

▶ starting pointer

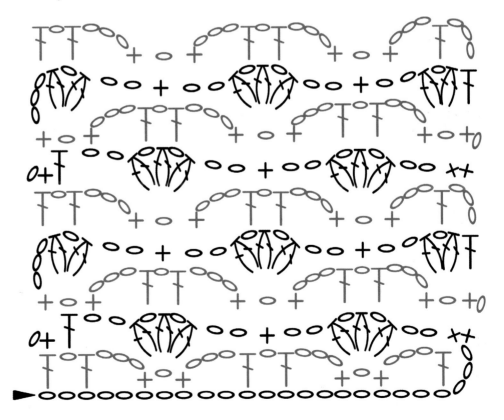

Mattress stitch seam

Using mattress stitch creates an invisible seam and I always use it for the top opening of pillows, although for the side and bottom seams it can be easier to use an overcast stitch (see Workshop 2, Joining squares: Overcast method, page 37). The overcast seam is a flat seam and quick to work but is worked from the wrong side so you need to turn the pillow cover right side out afterward. So to sew the final seam of the pillow cover follow these simple steps for mattress stitch, which is worked with right side facing.

(see Workshop 2, Joining squares: Overcast method, page 37)

Mattress stitch is made by picking up the loops or bars, either one stitch in or at the inside edge of the edging stitch of the first crochet piece, and then picking up the bars from the corresponding stitch on the second piece. If you're sewing together a piece without uniform stitches—such as on our Textured Pillow cover—it's not always obvious where to put the needle. If you're sewing up a piece crocheted in single crochet or double crochet—something that is uniform in shape—it's easier to see where the bars are.

> **TIP**
> Do not worry if you feel you're not picking up the right stitch—as long as you are placing your needle to the side of the edging stitch the seam will work out and look neat.

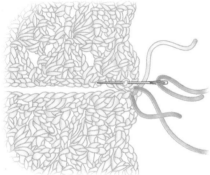

1 Line up the two pieces—pin them together if it helps make them more secure. Thread a tail of yarn in the same color as the pieces you're joining into a yarn sewing needle. Pick up a loop on the other side with the yarn sewing needle at a horizontal angle (90 degree angle) to the pattern and draw the yarn through loosely.

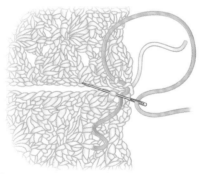

2 Pick up a loop on the corresponding side of the other piece just inside the edge and draw through the yarn. Leave the loops loose and don't draw them through tightly.

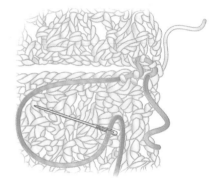

3 Pick up the next loop approx. ½ in. (1 cm) along on the same side and draw through the yarn.

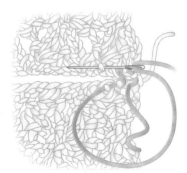

4 Pick up a loop on the corresponding side of the other piece just inside the edge and draw through the yarn. Leave the loops loose and don't draw them through tightly.

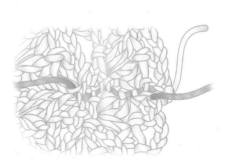

5 Repeat steps 3 and 4. When you have about 6 loops, hold the pieces firmly in place and pull the thread to draw the loose loops and bind the edging together.

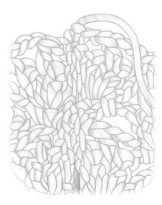

6 Continue in this way, repeating steps 3, 4, and 5 until the pillow cover top seam is joined. This will create an invisible seam on the right side of the work.

Large daisy

This 11-petal daisy flower uses two colors, one for the center and one for the petals. It is used on the Textured Pillow cover in this Workshop and also on the Shelf Edging in Workshop 13 (page 109), but it can also be the ideal embellishment for other crochet projects.

Foundation ring: Using a US size D-3 (3 mm) hook and A (yellow), make 6ch and join with a ss in first ch to form a ring.
Round 1 (RS): 1ch (counts as 1sc), 10sc in ring, join with a ss in first ch. *11 sts.*
Fasten off A.
Round 2 (RS): With RS facing, using B (off-white) and working in front loop only of each sc, join yarn with a ss in any st in Round 1, *6ch, 1hdc in 3rd ch from hook, 1dc in each of next 2 ch, 1sc in next ch, 1ss in same front loop as last ss was worked, 1ss in front loop of next sc of Round 1; rep from *, ending with 1ss in same front loop as first ss of round. *11 petals.*
Fasten off.

11-petal daisy chart

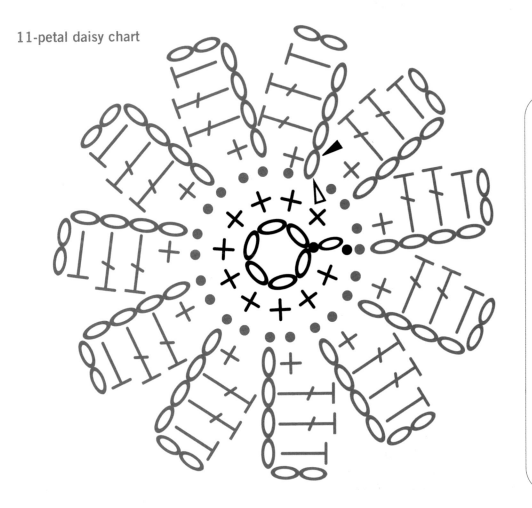

key	
◯	**ch** chain
•	**ss** slip stitch
+	**sc** single crochet
⊤	**dc** double crochet
⊤	**hdc** half double crochet
▶	starting pointer
▷	ending pointer

Textured Pillow

This is a great introduction to making textured stitches. Made using clusters and a thick chunky yarn, this pillow cover is embellished with a delicate eleven-petal daisy.

techniques used

Stitches—double crochet, half double crochet, trebles

Working a textured stitch

Making a two-double crochet cluster

Making an 11-petal daisy

Working an overcast seam

Working a mattress-stitch seam

Using flowers to adorn home projects

pillow cover measurements

Finished pillow cover fits a pillow form 16 in. (40 cm) square.

yarns

Pillow cover:
Debbie Bliss Rialto Chunky (100% extra-fine merino wool superwash) bulky- (chunky-) weight yarn

8 x 1¾oz (50g) balls—approx. 524yd (480m)—of main color:

MC 007 Gold (golden yellow)

Flowers:
Rowan Cotton Glacé (100% cotton) lightweight (light worsted) yarn

Small amounts in two contrasting colors:

A 856 Mineral (golden yellow)
B 725 Ecru (off-white)

hook

US size E-4 (3.5 mm) crochet hook
US size D-3 (3 mm) crochet hook

extras

16 in. (40 cm) square pillow form

gauge

15 sts x 8 rows over a 4 in. (10 cm) square worked in double crochet using a US size E-4 (3.5 mm) hook and MC.

abbreviations

ch	chain
cont	continu(e)ing
dc	double crcohet
MC	main color
rep	repeat
RS	right side
sc	single crochet
sp(s)	space(s)
ss	slip stitch
st(s)	stitch(es)
WS	wrong side
yoh	yarn over hook

special abbreviation

2dcCL (2-double crochet cluster): [Yoh and insert hook in sp (or st), yoh and pull yarn through work, yoh and pull yarn through first 2 loops on hook] twice in same sp/st (3 loops now on hook), yoh and pull yarn through all 3 loops on hook to complete the 2dcCL.

To make the pillow-cover front

Foundation chain: Using a US size E-4 (3.5 mm) hook and MC, make 74ch.

Row 1 (WS): 1dc in 4th ch from hook, *3ch, skip 2 ch, 1sc in next ch, 1ch, skip 1 ch, 1sc in next ch, 3ch, skip 2 ch, 1dc in next ch, 1ch, skip 1 ch, 1dc in next ch; rep from * to end.

Row 2 (RS): 1ch, 1sc in first dc, 1dc in first 1-ch sp (between first 2 dc), 2ch, *skip next 3-ch sp, [2dcCL, 1ch, 2dcCL, 1ch, 2dcCL] all in next 1-ch sp (between 2 sc), 2ch, skip next 3-ch sp**, 1sc in next 1-ch sp (between 2 dc), 2ch; rep from * ending last rep at **, skip last dc, 2sc in top of 3-ch at end of row.

Row 3 (WS): 1ch, 1sc in first sc, 1ch, skip next sc, 1sc in next 2-ch sp, *3ch, skip next 2dcCL, 1dc in next 1-ch sp (between 2dcCLs), 1ch, skip next 2dcCL, 1dc in next 1-ch sp (between 2dcCLs), 3ch, 1sc in next 2-ch sp, 1ch**, 1sc in next 2-ch sp; rep from * ending last rep at **, 1sc in last sc.

Row 4 (RS): 3ch, [2dcCL, 1ch, 2dcCL] all in first 1-ch sp (between 2 sc), 2ch, skip next 3-ch sp, 1sc in next 1-ch sp, (between 2 dc), 2ch, *skip next 3-ch sp, [2dcCL, 1ch, 2dcCL, 1ch, 2dcCL] all in next 1-ch sp (between 2 sc), 2ch, skip next 3-ch sp, 1sc in next 1-ch sp (between 2 dc), 2ch; rep from * to last 3-ch sp, skip last 3-ch sp, [2dcCL, 1ch, 2dcCL] all in next 1-ch sp (between last 2 sc), 1dc in last sc.

Row 5 (WS): 3ch, 1dc in first 1-ch sp (between 2dcCLs), 3ch, 1sc in next 2-ch sp, 1ch, 1sc in next 2-ch sp, *3ch, skip next 2dcCL, 1dc in next 1-ch sp (between 2dcCLs), 1ch, skip next 2dcCL, 1dc in next 1-ch sp (between 2dcCLs), 3ch, 1sc in next 2-ch sp, 1ch, 1sc in next 2-ch sp; rep from *, ending 3ch, skip next 2dcCL, 1dc in next 1-ch sp (between 2dcCLs), 1ch, 1dc in top of 3-ch at end of row.

Rep Rows 2–5 until work measures approximately 16 in. (40 cm), ending on a Row 2—about 42 rows will have been worked.

Fasten off.

Texture pattern chart

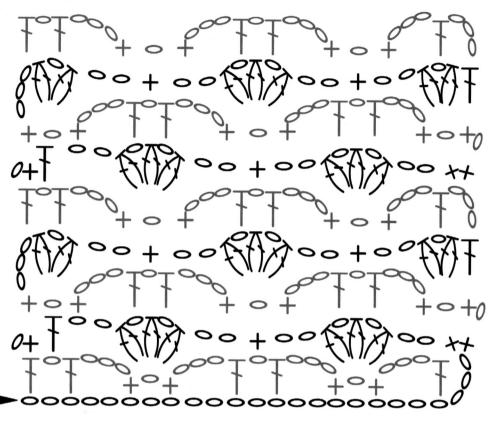

11-petal daisy chart

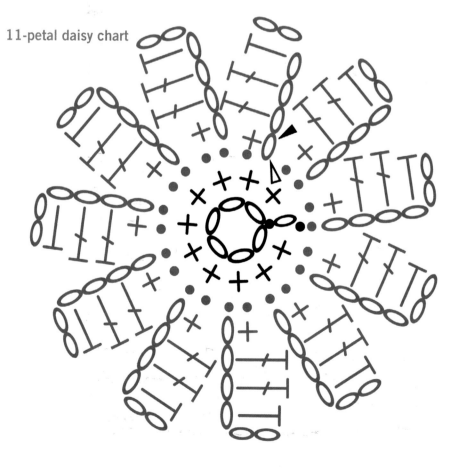

key

○   **ch**   chain

•   **ss**   slip stitch

+   **sc**   single crochet

⊤   **dc**   double crochet

T   **hdc**   half double crochet

⟨⟩   **2dcCL**   two-double crochet cluster

▶   starting pointer

▷   ending pointer

To make the pillow-cover back
Make exactly as for the front.

To make the daisy
Foundation ring: Using a US size D-3 (3 mm) hook and A (yellow), make 6ch and join with a ss in first ch to form a ring.
Round 1 (RS): 1ch (counts as 1sc), 10sc in ring, join with a ss in first ch. *11 sts.*
Fasten off A.
Round 2 (RS): With RS facing, using B (off-white) and working in front loop only of each sc, join yarn with a ss in any st in Round 1, *6ch, 1hdc in 3rd ch from hook, 1dc in each of next 2 ch, 1sc in next ch, 1ss in same front loop as last ss was worked, 1ss in front loop of next sc of Round 1; rep from *, ending with 1ss in same front loop as first ss of round. *11 petals.*
Fasten off.

To finish the cover
Using a yarn sewing needle, sew in all yarn ends on the crochet pieces.
Pin the pillow-cover front and the pillow-cover back with right sides together, matching rows and leaving the top edge open. Sew the seam together along the three pinned edges, using a yarn sewing needle and overcast stitch. Turn the cover right side out, insert the pillow form, pin the top edges together, and sew along the top using the mattress stitch joining method.
Sew the daisy to the center front of the pillow.

Workshop 6

Spirals and Rib

In this Workshop we cover working rounds in spirals, making a crochet rib with raised doubles, and making pompoms, all of which are put into practice in the project, a Bobble Hat. The other techniques in this Workshop are front and back raised doubles and using stitch markers, as well as working with chunky yarn and a large hook.

Working in spirals

When working crochet in rounds you can either join each round with a ss (see Workshop 3, Working in the round, page 42), or by continuing to crochet at the end of each round without joining, which creates a spiral.

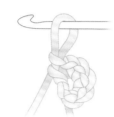

1 Spirals are started in a different way to the circles in Workshop 3; instead of creating a ring joined with a ss (see page 34), you make 2 chains and then make a group of stitches into the second ch from the hook, which creates a fan effect and is the beginning of the spiral.

2 Insert a strand of contrast yarn as a stitch marker in the loop on the hook when you have finished making the first stitches to mark the beginning of the round. Pop the strands of the stitch marker to sit at the back of the loop—or you can use a commercial bought stitch marker. The start of the round will be made into the first st.

Stitch markers

There are commercial stitch markers available on the market, made of plastic or metal. Some are decorative and have little beads at the end and the plastic ones can look like little safety pins or hooks (see page 15). I find using a contrasting piece of yarn a much better option that works for me as I tend to lose the tiny plastic ones down the back of my chair or sofa, but it doesn't matter if you lose a piece of yarn—you can just cut another piece. Cut a piece of yarn about 4 in. (10 cm) long in a contrasting color and loop the strand into the loop on your hook at the beginning/end of each round. Complete the round as instructed and the stitch that has the stitch marker in will be the last stitch that you go into. As soon as you have made this last stitch, move the stitch marker up to the loop on the hook and commence the next round.

> **TIP**
> Make sure you count the stitches at the end of every round when working in spirals and make sure the stitch marker strand is long enough and doesn't fall out of its stitch.

Creating crochet rib

Ribbing is more common in knitting, but you can also achieve a rib effect in crochet, and one method is to make a raised stitch as on our Bobble Hat.

Raised stitches are created by making stitches around the "posts" (also called "stalks" or "stems") of the stitches below (in the previous round/row).

Raised double round front (dc/rf)

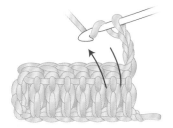  

1 Yarn over hook and insert the hook from the front and around the post (the stem) of the next double crochet from right to left.

2 Yarn over hook and pull the yarn through the work, yarn over hook and pull the yarn through the first 2 loops on the hook.

3 Yarn over hook and pull the yarn through the 2 loops on the hook (1 loop on hook). One raised double round front completed.

raised double round front (dc/rf) in symbols

Raised double round back (dc/rb)

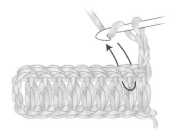 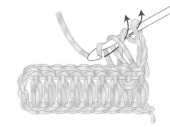 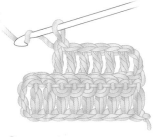

1 Yarn over hook and insert the hook from the back and around the post (the stem) of the next double crochet as directed in the pattern from right to left.

2 Yarn over hook and pull the yarn through the work, yarn over hook and pull the yarn through the first 2 loops on the hook.

3 Yarn over hook and pull the yarn through the 2 loops on the hook (1 loop on hook). One raised double round back completed.

raised double round back (dc/rb) in symbols

To practice front and back raised doubles

Make 13 ch,
Row 1: 1hdc in third ch from hook, 1hdc in each ch to end.
Row 2: 1dc/rf (round front) around each hdc to end.
Rows 3, 4, 5: 1dc/rb (round back) around each raised double from previous row to end.
Fasten off.

Raised doubles chart

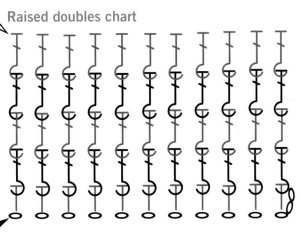

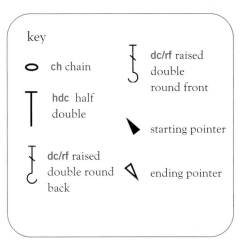

key

○ **ch** chain

⊤ **hdc** half double

dc/rf raised double round back

dc/rf raised double round front

► starting pointer

◁ ending pointer

Using bulky yarns and large hooks

The pattern for this Workshop uses a bulky yarn and a larger than average hook size. Crochet in the same way, but if you are finding it difficult to hold the hook in the usual way (see Getting started, Holding your hook, page 16), you may find it easier to hold the hook from the top, like you would hold a knife.

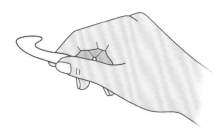

The definition of a bulky yarn is a yarn that is thicker than the average light worsted (double knit/DK) or worsted (Aran) thickness of yarn (see Getting Started, Standard Yarn Weight, page 10). Bulky yarns are great for making scarves, thick sweaters, or winter blankets. I often recommend using them in my scarf and hat projects for beginners because they crochet up really quickly, and also because the stitches are bigger and made with thicker hooks so it's easier to see each individual stitch. When my daughter first started to crochet, she made about ten scarves, all in different colors, for her friends as presents one Christmas, which went down very well and looked very impressive.

Pompoms

There are several different methods of making pompoms. You can buy commercial pompom makers in different sizes or you can use one of the homemade methods, in which case you can make your pompom any size you like.

Making pompoms: Cardboard circle method

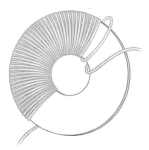

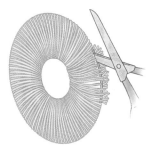

1 Draw around something with a diameter of about 4 in. (10 cm) onto two pieces of stiff cardboard (a cereal carton works well). Draw a smaller circle inside (draw around a large button or a cotton reel). Cut out the larger circle then cut out the inner circle. Keep the two circles held together and wrap the yarn through the ring, wrapping it closely together. Don't wrap it too tightly or it will be difficult to slide in the scissors to cut.

2 When it is closely packed with yarn all the way around, carefully cut through the wraps of yarn around the edge of the rings. Slide a length of yarn between the rings and tie it very tightly with a knot to hold all the strands together. Remove the rings of the pompom maker and fluff up the pompom. You can trim any straggly ends with scissors to make a neat ball.

Making pompoms: Book method

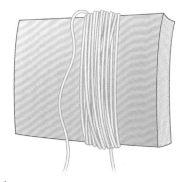

1 Leaving a long tail, wrap the yarn around a paperback book (or something a similar size) about 120 times, leaving a second long tail.

2 Ease the wrapped yarn off the book gently and wrap the second tail tightly around the center six or seven times.

3 Take a yarn sewing needle and thread in the second tail. Push needle through the center wrap backward and forward three or four times.

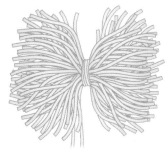

4 Cut the loops on each side of the wrap. Holding the two tails in one hand, hold the bobble and fluff it out.

5 Hold the bobble in one hand and use sharp scissors to trim it into a round and even shape.

Pompom Beanie Hats

These hats can be made in an evening and make great gifts. As I was making them for this book, I was asked to make another one each time someone visited! You'll need a stitch marker for this project, but if you don't have one, just use a short length of contrasting yarn. If making the hat for yourself, try it on for size as you go and either add more rows or omit Round 16(17:17) to make it shorter.

techniques used

Stitches—half double crochet, raised double crochet

Working with bulky yarn and a large hook

Making a hat in a spiral

Using stitch markers

Increasing with half double crochet

Reading a crochet pattern with different sizes

Making a crochet rib (raised doubles)

Making a pompom

hat sizes

Small (medium:large) adult hat sizes

To fit head circumference
21¼–21¾(22–22½:22¾–23¼) in./
54–55(56–57:58–59) cm

hat measurements

Small: The brim is approximately 20 in. (50 cm) in circumference, and the hat measures approximately 7½ in. (19 cm) from the edge of the brim (folded up) to the center top.

Medium: The brim is approximately 22 in. (55 cm) in circumference, and the hat measures approximately 7¾ in. (20 cm) from the edge of the brim (folded up) to the center top.

Large: The brim is approximately 24 in. (60 cm) in circumference, and the hat measures approximately 7¾ in. (20 cm) from the edge of the brim (folded up) to the center top.

Note: Instructions for the small size come first and those for the medium and large sizes follow inside parentheses; if there is only one figure, it applies to all sizes.

yarns

Debbie Bliss Paloma (60% alpaca, 40% wool) super-chunky- (super-bulky-) weight yarn

One-color red hat:
2(3:3) x 1¾oz (50g) hanks—approx. 142(213:213)yd/130(195:195)m—of main color:
MC 15 Ruby (red)

1 x 1¾oz (50g) hank—approx. 71yd/65m—of a contrasting color for pompom:
CC 24 Silver (gray)

One-color gray hat:
2(3:3) x 1¾oz (50g) hanks—approx. 142(213:213)yd/130(195:195)m—of main color:
MC 24 Silver (gray)

1 x 1¾oz (50g) hank—approx. 71yd/65m—of a contrasting color for pompom:
CC 15 Ruby (red)

Two-color white hat with blue brim:
2 x 1¾oz (50g) hanks—approx. 142yd/130m—of main color:
MC 01 Ecru (white)

2 x 1¾oz (50g) hanks—approx. 142yd/130m—of a contrasting color for brim and pompom:
CC 25 Soft Green (pale blue)

Two-color blue hat with green brim:
2 x 1¾oz (50g) hanks—approx. 142yd/130m—of main color:
MC 25 Soft Green (pale blue)

2 x 1¾oz (50g) hanks—approx. 142yd/130m—of a contrasting color for brim and pompom:
CC 26 Lime (light green)

hook

US size J-10 (6 mm) crochet hook

gauge

11 sts x 9 rows over a 4 in. (10 cm) square worked in half double crochet using a US size J-10 (6mm) hook.

abbreviations

beg	begin(ning)
CC	contrasting color
ch	chain
cont	continu(e)(ing)
dc	double crochet
hdc	half double
MC	main color
rep	repeat
RS	right side
ss	slip stitch
st(s)	stitch(es)
WS	wrong side
yoh	yarn over hook

special abbreviations

dc/rf (raised double crochet round front): yoh, insert hook from the front and around the post (the stem) of next dc from right to left, yoh, pull yarn through the work, [yoh, pull yarn through first 2 loops on hook] twice to complete the raised double round front.

dc/rb (raised double crochet round back): yoh, insert hook from the back and around the post (the stem) of next dc from right to left, yoh, pull yarn through the work, [yoh, pull yarn through first 2 loops on hook] twice to complete the raised double round back.

Notes

• The hat is started at the center top and worked downward in a spiral toward the brim edge.

• Mark the beginning (and end) of each round by inserting a stitch marker in the loop on the hook at the beginning of each round of the hat section, and in front of the raised double on the brim section.

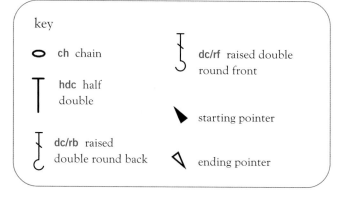

To make the hat

Using MC, begin hat at center top as follows:

Round 1 (RS): Make 2ch, then work 10hdc in 2nd ch from hook. *10 hdc.*

Mark the beginning of each round and cont in rounds with RS always facing you.

Round 2: Skip 2-ch at beg of round, 2hdc in each hdc to end. *20 hdc.*

Remember to keep moving the marker to mark the beginning of each round.

Round 3: *1hdc in next hdc, 2hdc in next hdc; rep from * to end. *30 hdc.*

Large size only

Round –(–:4): *1hdc in each of next 4 hdc, 2hdc in next hdc; rep from * to end. *–(–:36) hdc.*

All sizes

Round 4(4:5): *1hdc in each of next 5 hdc, 2hdc in next hdc; rep from * to end. *35(35:42) hdc.*

Round 5(5:6): *1hdc in each of next 6 hdc, 2hdc in next hdc; rep from * to end. *40(40:48) hdc.*

Round 6(6:7): *1hdc in each of next 7 hdc, 2hdc in next hdc; rep from * to end. *45(45:54) hdc.*

Round 7(7:8): *1hdc in each of next 8 hdc, 2hdc in next hdc; rep from * to end. *50(50:60) hdc.*

Medium size only

Round –(8:–): *1hdc in each of next 9 hdc, 2hdc in next hdc; rep from * to end. *–(55:–) hdc.*

All sizes

Rounds 8(9:9)–16(17:17): 1hdc in each hdc to end. *50(55:60) hdc.*

Brim

For a one-color hat, cont in MC. For a two-color hat, cut off MC now and join in CC for the next round.

Brim round 1: 1hdc in each hdc to end.

Keep the RS of the hat facing as you work the brim. As it is later turned up, the WS of the brim will be facing you as you work it.

Brim round 2: 1dc/rf (round *front*) around each hdc to end.

Brim rounds 3, 4, and 5: 1 dc/rb (round *back*) around each raised dc to end.

Brim round 6: 1dc/rb around each raised dc to last st, join with a ss around last st.

Fasten off.

There will be 4 raised "ribs" on the WS of the brim.

Turn the brim up so the right side of the brim is showing on the right side of the hat.

To finish the hat

Using a yarn sewing needle, sew in all yarn ends—as you do this, neaten the join at the last brim stitch and the ring at the center of the top of the hat.

Press the brim carefully using a damp cloth, ensuring that it's neat and straight.

To make the pompom

Using CC, make one large pompom with the remaining yarn (see pages 64–65). Trim the pompom to approximately 3 in. (7.5 cm) diameter and then sew it to the top of the hat.

Brim chart

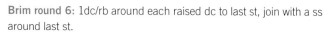

key	
⬭ **ch** chain	⅂ **dc/rf** raised double round front
⊤ **hdc** half double	▶ starting pointer
⅂ **dc/rb** raised double round back	◁ ending pointer

Workshop 7

Making a Garment

Crocheting a garment can be very daunting; it's a larger project than accessories and there is some shaping to handle as well as sewing the pieces together. For this Workshop project I've created a Basic Sweater with very simple shaping, using increases and decreases in half double crochet—half double two stitches together (hdc2tog) (decreases) and 2hdc in the same stitch (increases). The garment is made in basic half double crochet with single crochet for the cuffs and the bottom welt (a welt is a panel at the bottom of the sweater in a different stitch to help retain the shape and structure of the garment).

Understanding measurements

When making a chain ring you usually start with 4–6 chains, depending on how much space you need inside the ring to make the stitches in the next round.

Bust measurement: for this project, the measurement is taken from the finished garment all the way round from armpit to armpit. It's the finished measurement not the actual bust size.

Length from shoulder: this measurement is taken from the shoulder to the bottom edge of the sweater.

Sleeve length: The sweater in this Workshop has a "dropped sleeve"—this is the simplest of sleeves to make and the join of the sleeve starts at the armpit. The measurement is taken from the armpit to the bottom edge of the cuff.

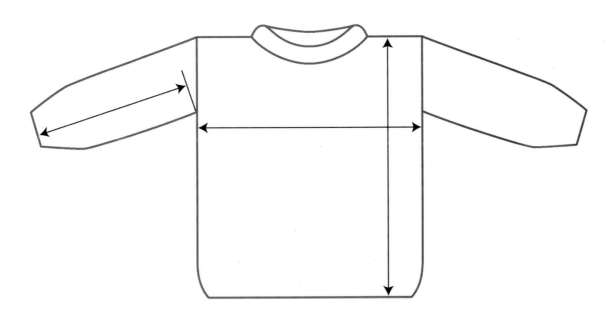

Changing the length of the front, back or sleeve

If you would like to make a longer or shorter body or sleeve, then simply stop crocheting (for shorter garment) or add more rows (for longer garment) to adjust the given measurements for the length before the shoulder or sleeve shapings in the pattern. The area between the dotted lines is where you can adjust—but remember to make identical changes on both sleeves so they will match, and to repeat any changes made on the back piece on the front piece(s) also.

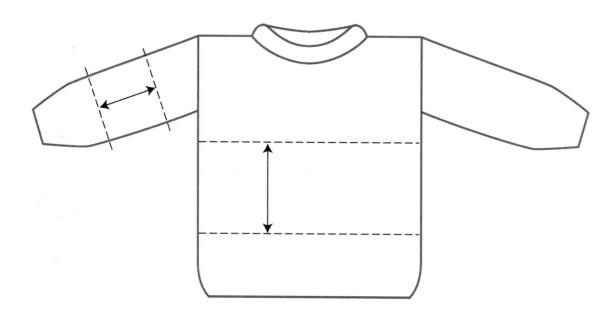

Half double crochet two stitches together (hdc2tog)—Decreases

half double crochet two stitches together (hdc2tog) in symbols

1 Yarn over hook, insert the hook into the next stitch, yarn over hook, pull the yarn through the work (3 loops on hook).

2 Yarn over hook, insert the hook into the next stitch, yarn over hook, pull the yarn through the work (5 loops on hook).

3 Yarn over hook, pull the yarn through all five loops on the hook (1 loop on hook). One half double two stitches together made.

Necks

In the pattern in this Workshop the neck is made by picking up the stitches around the shoulders, front and back neck edges of the garment pieces. The pattern tells you how many stitches to pick up across each piece around the first round.

A neckband is then crocheted on these stitches and is made tall enough to fold over on itself so that you can loosely sew down the edge to the garment to create a neat and tidy finish.

Sewing pieces together

Sewing garment pieces together is something many people avoid. When I started out knitting and crocheting I used to get my mother to sew up my garments after I made them—I was too frightened of messing it all up. But with a little confidence you'll get the perfect seams and realize there is really nothing complicated about it at all.

The secret is to pin the seams together before you start sewing with the yarn sewing needle. Make sure you have right sides together, use large plastic headed pins and pin just below the edge of the seam. Use your preferred joining stitch—for garments, I usually use the overcast joining method with the right sides together (see Workshop 2, Joining squares: Overcast method on page 37). When you start to sew, match the stitches on each of the edges of the seams stitch by stitch.

If possible it is also best to block your garment pieces out first (see Getting started, Blocking, steaming and pressing, page 27). The yarn I've used in the project for this Workshop does not require blocking because it is firm and doesn't curl at the edges. If you are using a softer wool, blocking will help considerably.

TIP
I have often sewn a wrong side to a right side by mistake and had to undo my work. Make sure you have right sides of your pieces together so that you're sewing up on the wrong side of the work and check and check again before beginning to sew. When fitting pieces together use stitch markers, pins or safety pins to indicate the center of each piece so you can match them evenly.

Reading from a pattern with different sizes

When making garments from a pattern that covers several different sizes you will find that the different sizes are shown throughout the pattern using brackets and colons. The smallest size is shown first, followed by the larger sizes inside the brackets and separated by colons. For example: Make 66(72:74:76:80:84) ch. The amount of yarn for the project may also change depending on the size—the larger sizes will use up more yarn. This is also shown in the materials list in the pattern in the same way, for example: 9(9:10:10:11:11) x 50g balls.

When you're in the middle of reading a pattern as you make the garment, all these different figures can sometimes be confusing. I always use a highlighter pen to mark the size that I'm following throughout the pattern before I begin. Or, if I can't find a highlighter pen, I circle my size with a pen or pencil.

Basic Sweater

If you've been waiting for a basic sweater pattern, here it is. This is such a great project for any level. I have added stripes here and there, but to make it your own, simply add a contrasting color to the sleeves or neck or anywhere else! I also made the sleeves three-quarter length; if you want them longer see page 70.

techniques used

Stitches—single crochet, half double crochet

Making a basic sweater

Changing colors for stripes

Shaping necks and sleeves

Decreasing using half double crochet

Increasing using half double crochet

Adjusting sleeve length on simple sleeves

Joining garment pieces together

sweater sizes

To fit women's sizes:

8	10	12	14	16	18

measurements

Around bust

in.	40	43½	45	46	48½	51
cm	100	109	112	115	122	128

Length from shoulder

in.	24	24	26½	26½	27½	27½
cm	61	61	67	67	70	70

Sleeve length

in.	13½	13½	15	16	16	16
cm	34.5	34.5	38	40.5	40.5	40.5

Note: The sleeve length is adjustable.

yarns

Debbie Bliss *Donegal Luxury Tweed Aran* (90% wool, 10% angora) Aran- (worsted-) weight yarn

9(9:10:10:11:11) x 1¾oz (50g) balls—approx. 864(864:960:960:1056:1056)yd/ 792(792:880:880:968:968)m—of main color:

MC 10 Silver (light gray)

1(1:1:1:1 x 1¾oz (50g) ball—approx. 96yd/88m—of each of two contrasting colors:

A 21 Fuchsia
B 37 Tangerine (orange)

hook

US size I-9 (5.5 mm) crochet hook
US size H-8 (5 mm) crochet hook

gauge

13 sts x 11 rows over a 4 in. (10 cm) square worked in half double crochet using a US size I-9 (5.5 mm) hook or appropriate hook to achieve correct gauge.

abbreviations

beg	beginning
ch	chain
cont	continu(e)(ing)
foll	following
hdc	half double
inc	increase
MC	main color
rep	repeat
RS	right side
sc	single crochet
ss	slip stitch
st(s)	stitch(es)
tog	together
yoh	yarn over hook

special abbreviation

hdc2tog (half double 2 together decrease): [Yoh, insert hook in next st, yoh and pull yarn through work] twice (5 loops now on hook), yoh, pull yarn through all 5 loops on hook to complete the hdc2tog decrease.

To make the sweater back

Welt

The welt is a border at the bottom of the garment, which is often a different stitch to the stitch used in the main section. It holds the shape of the bottom edge of the garment nicely.

Foundation chain: Using a US size I-9 (5.5 mm) hook and MC, make 66(72:74:76:80:84)ch.

Row 1 (RS): 1sc in 2nd ch from hook, 1sc in each ch to end. *65(71:73:75:79:83) sc.*

Change to a US size H-8 (5 mm) hook.

Row 2: 1ch (does not count as a st), 1sc in each sc to end.

Rep Row 2 six times more, so ending with a WS row.

Main body

Change to a US size I-9 (5.5 mm) hook.

Row 1 (RS): 2ch (counts as first hdc), skip first sc, 1hdc in each sc to end. *65(71:73:75:79:83) sts.*

Cut off MC and change to A.

Row 2: Using A, 2ch (counts as first hdc), skip first hdc, 1hdc in next hdc and in each hdc to end, 1hdc in top of 2-ch at end of row.

Cut off A and change to MC.

Row 3: Using MC, 2ch (counts as first hdc), skip first hdc, 1hdc in next hdc and in each hdc to end, 1hdc in top of 2-ch at end of row.

Cut off MC and change to B.

Row 4: Using B, 2ch (counts as first hdc), skip first hdc, 1hdc in next hdc and in each hdc to end, 1hdc in top of 2-ch at end of row.

TIPS

• Changing colors: When changing colors, just before you work the last step (the last yoh) of the last stitch of the row using the old yarn, drop the old yarn and pick up the new yarn, wrap it over the hook and pull it through to complete the last stitch of the row—this joins in the new yarn.

• Sewing garment seams: Leave a long length of the yarn before joining in a new color—this strand can be used to sew side and sleeve seams.

Cut off B and change to MC.

Row 5: Using MC, 2ch (counts as first hdc), skip first hdc, 1hdc in next hdc and in each hdc to end, 1hdc in top of 2-ch at end of row.**

Using MC only, cont in hdc as set until Back measures 23¼(23¼:25¾:25¾:26¾:26¾) in./59(59:65:65:68:68) cm from beg of welt, ending on a WS row.

Shape right back neck

Next row (RS): 2ch (counts as first hdc), skip first hdc, 1hdc in each of next 24(27:28:28:30:31) hdc, 1sc in each of next 2 hdc, turn.

Next row: 1ss in each of first 2 sc, 1sc in each of next 2 hdc, 1hdc in each hdc to end, 1hdc in top of 2-ch at end of row. *23(26:27:27:29:30) hdc.*
Fasten off.

Shape left back neck

With RS facing and using a US size I-9 (5.5 mm) and MC, return to last complete row worked, skip next 11(11:11:13:13:15) hdc at center, rejoin yarn with a ss to foll hdc, 1ch, 1sc in same place as ss, 1sc in next hdc, 1hdc in each hdc to end, 1hdc in top of 2-ch at end of row. *25(28:29:29:31:32) hdc.*

Next row: 2ch (counts as first hdc), skip first hdc, 1hdc in each st to last 2 hdc, 1sc in each of last 2 hdc.
Fasten off.

To make the sweater front

Work as for Back to **.

Using MC only, cont in hdc as set until 4(4:4:4:4:4) rows fewer than on Back have been worked to beg of neck shaping, so ending with a WS row.

Shape left front neck

Next row (RS): 2ch (counts as first hdc), skip first hdc, 1hdc in each of next 26(29:30:30:32:33) hdc, 1sc in each of next 2 hdc, turn. *29(32:33:33:35:36) sts.*

Next row: 1ss in each of first 2 sc (do not count as sts), 1sc in each of next 2 hdc, 1hdc in each hdc to end, 1hdc in top of 2-ch at end of row. *27(30:31:31:33:34) sts.*

Next row: 2ch (counts as first hdc), skip first hdc, 1hdc in each hdc to last 2 hdc, hdc2tog over these last 2 hdc. *24(27:28:28:30:31) sts.*

Next row: 2ch (counts as first hdc), skip hdc2tog, hdc2tog over next 2 hdc, 1hdc in each st to end, 1hdc in top of 2-ch at end of row. *23(26:27:27:29:30) sts.*

Next 2 rows: 2ch, (counts as first hdc), skip first hdc, 1hdc in each hdc to end, 1hdc in top of 2-ch at end of row.
Fasten off.

Shape right front neck

With RS facing and using a US size I-9 (5.5 mm) hook and MC, return to last complete row worked, skip next 7(7:7:9:9:11) hdc at center, rejoin yarn with a ss to foll hdc, 1ch, 1sc in same place as ss, 1sc in next hdc, 1hdc in each hdc to end, 1hdc in top of 2-ch at end of row. *29(32:33:33:35:36) sts.*

Next row: 2ch (counts as first hdc), skip first hdc, 1hdc in

each hdc to last 2hdc, 1sc in each of last 2 hdc. *27(30:31:31:33:34) sts.*

Next row: 1ss in each of first 2 sc, hdc2tog over next 2 hdc, 1hdc in each hdc to end, 1hdc in top of 2-ch at end of row. *24(27:28:28:30:31) sts.*

Next row: 2ch (counts as first hdc), skip first hdc, 1hdc in each of next 20(23:24:24:26:27) hdc, hdc2tog over next 2 hdc, 1hdc in top of hdc2tog at end of row. *23(26:27:27:29:30) sts.*

Next 2 rows: 2ch (counts as first hdc), skip first hdc, 1hdc in each hdc to end, 1hdc in top of 2-ch at end of row.
Fasten off.

To make the sleeves

(Make two the same)

Cuff

Using a US size I-9 (5.5 mm) hook and MC, make 29(31:31:33:33:33) ch.

Row 1 (RS): 1sc in 2nd ch from hook, 1sc in each ch to end. *28(30:30:32:32:32) sc.*

Change to a US size H-8 (5 mm) hook.

Row 2: 1ch (does not count as a st), 1sc in each sc to end.
Rep Row 2 five times more, so ending with a RS row.

Next row (inc): 1ch, 1sc in each of first 2 sc, 2sc in next sc, 1sc in each of next 6(7:7:8:8:8) sc, 2sc in next sc, 1sc in each of next 8 sc, 2sc in next sc, 1sc in next 6(7:7:8:8:8) sc, 2sc in next sc, 1sc in each of last 2 sc. *32(34:34:36:36:36) sc.*

Main sleeve

Change to a US size I-9 (5.5 mm) hook.

Row 1 (RS): 2ch (counts as first hdc), skip first sc, 1hdc in each sc to end. *32(34:34:36:36:36) sts.*

Cut off MC and change to A.

Row 2: Using A, 2ch (counts as first hdc), skip first hdc, 1hdc in next hdc and each hdc to end, 1hdc in top of 2-ch at end of row.

Cut off A and change to MC.

Row 3 (inc): Using MC, 2ch (counts as first hdc), skip first hdc, 1hdc in next hdc, 2hdc in next hdc, 1hdc in each hdc to last 2 hdc, 2hdc in next hdc, 1hdc in last hdc, 1hdc in top of 2-ch at end of row. *34(36:36:38:38:38) sts.*

Cut off MC and change to B.

Row 4: Using B, 2ch (counts as first hdc), skip first hdc, 1hdc in next hdc and in each hdc to end, 1hdc in top of 2-ch at end of row.

Cut off B and change to MC.

Row 5: Using MC, 2ch (counts as first hdc), skip first hdc, 1hdc in next hdc and in each hdc to end, 1hdc in top of 2-ch at end of row.

Cont with MC only.

Row 6 (inc): 2ch (counts as first hdc), skip first hdc, 1hdc in next hdc, 2hdc in next hdc, 1hdc in each hdc to last 2 hdc, 2hdc in next hdc, 1hdc in last hdc, 1hdc in top of 2-ch at end of row. *36(38:38:40:40:40) sts.*

Rows 7 and 8: Rep Rows 5 and 6. *38(40:40:42:42:42) sts.*

SIZES 16 AND 18 ONLY

Rep Rows 5 and 6 four times more. *–(–:–:–:50:50) sts.*

Now work as from Row 9.

ALL SIZES

Rows 9, 10, and 11: 2ch (counts as first hdc), 1 hdc in next hdc and in each hdc to end, 1hdc in top of 2-ch at end of row.

Row 12 (inc): 2ch (counts as first hdc), skip first hdc, 1hdc in next hdc, 2hdc in next hdc, 1hdc in each hdc to last 2 hdc, 2hdc in next hdc, 1hdc in last hdc, 1hdc in top of 2-ch at end of row. *40(42:42:44:52:52) sts.*

Rep Rows 9–12 another 4(5:5:5:4:4) times. *48(52:52:54:60:60) sts.*

Work without shaping until Sleeve measures 13½(13½:15:16:16:16) in./34.5(34.5:38:40.5:40.5:40.5) cm from beg of cuff or desired length.

Fasten off.

To add the neckband

Join the shoulder seams.

With RS facing and using a US size H-8 (5 mm) hook and MC, join yarn with a ss at left shoulder seam, 1ch, then work 13(13:13:13:13:13)sc evenly down left front neck edge, 7(7:7:9:9:11)sc across center front neck sts, 13(13:13:13:13:13)sc evenly up right front neck edge, 25(25:25:27:27:29)sc evenly around back neck edge, join

with ss in first sc, do not turn. *58(58:58:62:62:66) sc.*

Round 1 (RS): 1ch (does not count as a st), 1sc in each sc to end, join with a ss in first sc of round.

Cont with RS always facing you.

Rep Round 1 six times more.

Fasten off.

To finish

Place markers along side seam edges of Front and Back 7¼(8:8:8¼:9½:9½) in./18.5(20:20:21:24:24) cm from shoulder seams. The sleeve tops fit between these markers. Place a marker at the center of the last row (top) of each Sleeve.

Laying the pieces on a flat surface, place one Sleeve on the Body with right sides together and matching the center of the top of the Sleeve to the shoulder seam. Using large plastic- or glass-headed pins, pin the top of the Sleeve to the Body between the markers. Sew the other Sleeve to the Body in the same way.

Sew the side and sleeve seams.

Fold the neckband over to the right side of the jumper so the first and last rows are aligned and pin—this makes the neckband a double thickness. Using a yarn sewing needle and overcast stitch (see Workshop 2, Joining squares: Overcast method, page 37), loosely stitch the neckband in place.

Sew in all yarn ends.

Workshop 8

Beading

This Workshop covers everything you need to know to add beads to your crochet: choosing beads, threading them onto the yarn and the beading technique. The project to put all this into practice is a Beaded Headband.

Beading

Beading is a great accessory but you must choose the right size of beads for the size of yarn you're working with. Many beads are made for fine threads and wires so the hole in the center of the bead is much too small for yarn.

Seed beads are most commonly used for yarn—they are shaped like little seeds. Size 6 is approximately 4mm in diameter and is a suitable size for light worsted (DK) and worsted (Aran) weight yarns. Size 8 is approximately 3mm in diameter and is suitable to use with fingering (4-ply or lace-weight) yarns.

Thread beads onto yarn

All the beads must be threaded onto the yarn before you start crocheting. If you run out of beads and need to add more, you will need to cut the yarn at the end of the row/round and thread more beads onto the ball and then join in the yarn again to continue.

The size of the hole in the bead is usually too small for a yarn sewing needle eye to go through, and the yarn is too thick to be threaded onto a normal sewing needle, so here is a technique to thread the beads onto the yarn.

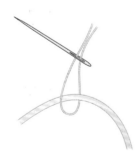

1 Make a loop with some cotton sewing thread and thread a sewing needle with the loop (not the end). Leave the loop hanging approx. 1 in. (2.5 cm) from the eye of the needle. Pull the yarn end through the loop of thread.

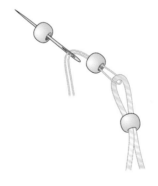

2 Thread the beads (two or three at a time), onto the sewing needle, pushing them down onto the strand of the yarn. Continue to thread beads until the required number is reached.

Beads are placed when working with the wrong side of the work facing you. The beads will sit at the back of the work, and so appear on the front (right side).

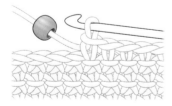

1 When a bead is needed, slide it up the strand toward the back of the work so it's ready to place in the right part of the stitch you're working (see page 78).

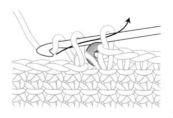

2 Work the stitch as indicated in the pattern. This will secure the bead at the back.

Beading charts

On a chart, the position of the bead is shown as a circle sitting on top of the stitch that it is placed with. On this chart, the bead is being placed with a single crochet stitch. If the beads are different colors to form a design, the bead circles may be colored on the chart to show which color goes where.

key

o   **ch** chain

+   **sc** single crochet

✛   **beaded sc** single crochet with bead

⋏   **sc2tog** single crochet 2 stitches together

≡   chart continues as set to length as specified in pattern

▶   starting pointer

▷   ending pointer

Beading chart

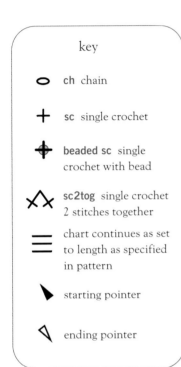

Beading with different stitches

Beads can be placed anywhere within the stitch depending on the design
and pattern. Most commonly the bead is placed near the top of the stitch.

Single crochet creates one of the most dense fabrics in crochet, which means the bead tends to sit on the outside of the fabric well. Half double and double crochets are a more open stitch and the bead is placed onto one of the strands near the top of the stitch and it tends to sit into the fabric more. When beading, make sure your gauge is not too loose, or the bead may get lost inside the fabric.

Placing a bead with single crochet

 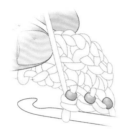

1 Insert the hook into the stitch, yarn over hook, pull the yarn through the stitch (2 loops on hook), slide the bead up the yarn strand so it is close to the back of the work.

2 Yarn over hook, pull the yarn through both loops on the hook. The bead is now placed at the back of the work.

Placing a bead with half double crochet

1 Yarn over hook, insert the hook into the stitch, yarn over hook, pull the yarn through stitch (3 loops on hook). Slide the bead up the yarn strand close to the back of the work.

2 Yarn over hook, pull the yarn through all 3 loops on the hook. The bead is now placed at the back of the work.

Placing a bead with double crochet

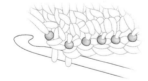 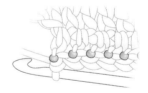

1 Yarn over hook, insert the hook into the stitch, yarn over hook, pull the yarn through the stitch (3 loops on hook), yarn over hook, pull the yarn through the first two loops on the hook (2 loops on hook). Slide the bead up the yarn strand and place it close to the back of the work.

2 Yarn over hook, pull the yarn through both loops on the hook. The bead is now placed at the back of the work.

TIP
When you are working with many beads in your design you may find you have made a mistake and missed one out. If so, then you can just sew the bead in the right place using a sewing needle and cotton thread.

Beaded Headband

Although it includes beading this is also a good project for practicing straight lines. Play around with the bead design—I've used just one color of bead, but you could have fun and use a variety of different colors, either at random or in a planned pattern.

techniques used

Stitches—single crochet

Choosing beads for crochet

Threading beads onto yarn

Increasing and decreasing with single crochet

Beading technique

headband measurements

Finished headband measures 2 in. (5 cm) wide x approximately 45 in. (114 cm) long.

yarn

Fyberspates *Vivacious 4-ply* (100% superwash merino) super-fine-weight (fingering) yarn

1 x 3½oz (100g) hank—approx. 399yd (365m)—of 611 Mixed Magentas (bright pink)

hook

US size G-6 (4 mm) crochet hook

extras

Approximately 635 round pale pink beads 4mm in diameter, such as Debbie Abraham Beads size 8 *Pink Seed Beads* (shade 333)

gauge

22 sts and 23 rows to a 4 in. (10 cm) square over single crochet bead pattern using a US size G-6 (4 mm) hook.

abbreviations

ch	chain
RS	right side
sc	single crochet
tog	together
WS	wrong side
yoh	yarn over hook
[]	repeat stitch sequence in brackets as many times as stated

special abbreviations

PB (place bead): *On a wrong-side row,* insert hook in next sc, yoh and pull yarn through (2 loops now on hook), slide bead up close to work, yoh and pull yarn through both loops on hook to complete beaded sc.

sc2tog (single crochet 2 together decrease): [Insert hook in next st, yoh and pull yarn through work] twice (3 loops now on hook), yoh and pull through all 3 loops on hook to complete the sc2tog decrease.

To make the headband

Thread beads onto yarn (see page 76).

Use single crochet throughout.

Foundation chain: Make 4ch.

Row 1 (WS): 1sc in 2nd ch from hook, PB in next ch, 1sc in next ch. *3 sc/1 bead.*

Row 2 (RS): 1ch (does not count as a st), 2sc in first sc, 1sc in next sc, 2sc in last sc. *5 sc.*

Row 3: 1ch, 1sc in first sc, [PB in next sc, 1sc in next sc] twice. *5 sc /2 beads.*

Row 4: 1ch, 2sc in first sc, 1sc in each of next 3 sc, 2sc in last sc. *7 sc.*

Row 5: 1ch, 1sc in first sc, [PB in next sc, 1sc in next sc] 3 times. *7 sc/3 beads.*

Row 6: 1ch, 2sc in next sc, 1sc in each of next 5 sc, 2sc in last sc. *9 sc.*

Row 7: 1ch, 1sc in first sc, [PB in next sc, 1sc in next sc] 4 times. *9 sc/4 beads.*

Row 8: 1ch, 2sc in next sc, 1sc in each of next 7 sc, 2sc in last sc. *11 sc.*

This completes the shaped end of the headband. Now work without shaping as follows:

Row 9: 1ch, 1sc in first sc, [PB in next sc, 1sc in next sc] 5 times. *11 sc/5 beads.*

Row 10: 1ch, 1sc in each sc to end. *11 sc.*

Rep Rows 9 and 10 until headband measures 43½ in. (110 cm) from beginning, ending on a Row 9 (a bead row).

Make sure you have 10 beads left for the last 9 rows.

Shape end

Now shape the end of the headband to match the first shaped end.

Next row: 1ch, sc2tog, 1sc in each of next 7 sc, sc2tog. *9 sc.*

Next row: 1ch, 1sc in first st, [PB in next sc, 1sc in next sc] 4 times. *9 sc/4 beads.*

Next row: 1ch, sc2tog, 1sc in each of next 5 sc, sc2tog. *7 sc.*

Next row: 1ch, 1sc in first sc, [PB in next sc, 1sc in next sc] 3 times. *7 sc/3 beads.*

Next row: 1ch, sc2tog, 1sc in each of next 3 sc, sc2tog. *5 sc.*

Next row: 1ch, 1sc in first sc, [PB in next sc, 1sc in next sc] twice. *5 sc/2 beads.*

Next row: 1ch, sc2tog, 1sc in next sc, sc2tog. *3 sc.*

Next row: 1ch, 1sc in first sc, PB in next sc, 1sc in last sc. *3 sc/1 bead.*

Next row: 1ch, sc2tog, 1sc in last sc. *2 sc.*

Fasten off.

To finish the headband

Using a yarn sewing needle, sew in any yarn ends.

Headband chart

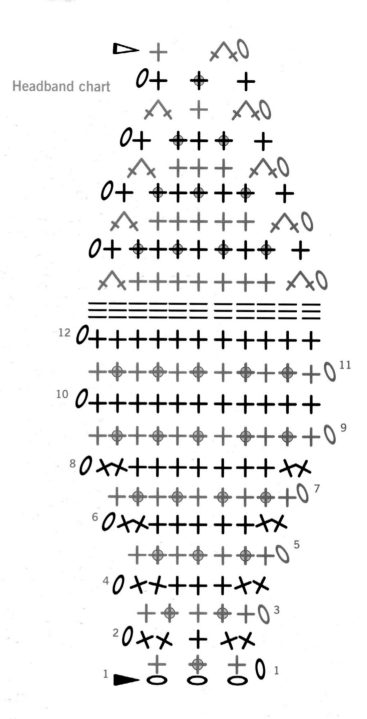

key

○ **ch** chain

+ **sc** single crochet

✛ **beaded sc** single crochet with bead

⋏⋋ **sc2tog** single crochet 2 stitches together

= **chart continues as set to length as specified in pattern**

▶ **starting pointer**

◁ **ending pointer**

Workshop 9

Hexagons

Hexagons start as circles and are made in rounds and you will always be working on the right side. The hexagons used in the project pattern for this Workshop are made using two double crochet clusters (see Workshop 5, page 54) and three double crochet clusters (see below), which form a petal-type design. The hexagon shape doesn't start until the third round. The Workshop also covers laying out and joining your hexagon motifs.

Three-double crochet cluster (3dcCL)

This cluster is made up of three doubles.

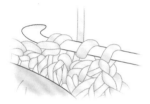

1 Yarn over hook, insert the hook in the stitch (or space).

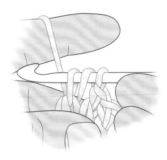

2 Yarn over hook, pull the yarn through the work (3 loops on hook).

3 Yarn over hook, pull the yarn through 2 loops on the hook (2 loops on hook).

4 Yarn over hook, insert the hook in the same stitch (or space).

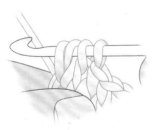

5 Yarn over hook, pull the yarn through the work (4 loops on hook).

6 Yarn over hook, pull the yarn through 2 loops on the hook (3 loops on hook).

7 Yarn over hook, insert the hook in the same stitch (or space), yarn over hook, pull the yarn through the work (5 loops on hook).

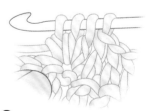

8 Yarn over hook, pull the yarn through 2 loops on the hook (4 loops on hook).

9 Yarn over hook, pull the yarn through all 4 loops on the hook (1 loop on hook). One three-double crochet cluster made.

three-double crochet cluster (3dcCL) in symbols

Hexagon motif

This hexagon motif is worked using three colors of yarn. For the project in this Workshop, the second color is always off-white (the main color) to make the design more cohesive since it contains so many hexagons, but if you are making a smaller item with hexagons you could use any three colors at random. See Workshop 5, page 54, for details of a two-double crochet cluster (2dcCL) stitch.

Foundation ring: Using first color, make 6ch and join with a ss in first chain to form a ring.
Round 1 (RS): 3ch, 2dcCL in ring, 2ch, [3dcCL in ring, 2ch] 5 times, join with a ss in 3rd of first 3-ch. *6 clusters.*
Fasten off.
Cont in rounds with RS always facing you.
Round 2: Join MC (off-white) with a ss in any 2-ch sp between any 3dcCL groups from previous Round, 3ch, [2dcCL, 2ch, 3dcCL] in same ch sp, *2ch, [3dcCL, 2ch, 3dcCL] in next 2-ch sp; rep from * 4 times more, 2ch, join with a ss in 3rd of first 3-ch. *12 clusters.*
Fasten off.

Round 3 (hexagon round): Join third color with a ss in 2-ch sp in middle of any "3dcCL, 2ch, 3dcCL" group, 3ch, [2dc, 2ch, 3dc] in same sp (corner), *3dc in next 2-ch sp, [3dc, 2ch, 3dc] in next ch sp (corner); rep from * 4 times more, 3dc in next ch sp, join with a ss in 3rd of first 3-ch. 6 corners.
Do not fasten off.
Round 4: Continue using same col, 1ch, 1sc in each of next 2 sts, 2sc in next ch sp (corner), *1sc in each of next 9 sts, 2sc in next ch sp (corner); rep from * 4 times more, 1sc in each of next 6 sts, join with a ss in top of first sc.
Fasten off.

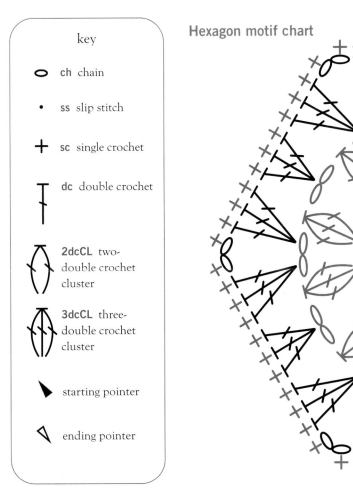

key	
⊙	**ch** chain
•	**ss** slip stitch
+	**sc** single crochet
┬	**dc** double crochet
⋀	**2dcCL** two-double crochet cluster
⋀	**3dcCL** three-double crochet cluster
▶	starting pointer
◁	ending pointer

Hexagon motif chart

Joining blanket motifs

When you have a variety of color combinations, it's important to lay out the motifs first so you can evenly place the colors in the blanket. Place the motifs in order on a flat surface, for example a table or a floor, preferably somewhere near where you are working so you don't have far to go when picking up pieces and returning to sit back down to crochet.

Also find a space that is not going to be disturbed—I have a cat and a dog so it's very difficult to lay pieces on the floor without either one of them walking across and disturbing the order I've laid them in.

You will often be asked to lay out motifs in a random order. However, you still need to space the colors evenly for a good effect and you can only do this by laying all the motifs out before you start joining and moving them around until you are happy. Otherwise set the motifs out in the order instructed.

For the Hexagon blanket project with this Workshop follow the chart below to set out the motifs. The hexagons are joined using a single crochet seam (see Workshop 3, single crochet seam, page 43). Make sure that the Hexagons are placed wrong sides together before joining because the single crochet seam shows a raised join on the right side of the work, which makes the hexagon shape and colors stand out.

Labeling blanket motifs

If you have to go away and leave your laid-out hexagons before you have joined them all up, it's vital to label them and if necessary pin them together.

Label the rows vertically and horizonally and make a mark on the label whether your row starts on the left (with an "L") or the right (with an "R"). I also use quilting pins (the bent safety pin type) to pin all the hexagons together if I think I'm going to have to move my piece—this ensures that the hexagons stay in the same order.

The joining of hexagons is a long process—it takes time and patience and there is no particular sequence to follow. However, the hexagons automatically fall into "flower" shapes and sometimes it's easier to join the hexagons into flowers and then join the flowers together.

Hexagon Blanket

This blanket is one of my favorite projects in the book; I love the simplicity, I love the yarn and the colors. Please play with the colors and choose them to suit your color scheme—but if you always use the same color for Round 2, it will really make the contrasting colors stand out.

techniques used

Stitches—single crochet, double crochet

Making a hexagon

Making clusters

Joining squares with single crochet seams

blanket measurements

Finished blanket measures approximately 46 x 46 in. (177 x 177 cm).

yarns

Debbie Bliss *Baby Cashmerino* (55% merino wool, 33% microfiber, 12% cashmere) lightweight (sport-weight) yarn

9 x 1¾oz (50g) balls—approx. 1233yd (1125m)—of main color:

MC 101 Ecru (off-white)

3 x 1¾oz (50g) balls—approx. V (375m)—each of five colors:

A 083 Butter (yellow)
B 202 Light Blue (pale blue)
C 068 Peach Melba (peach)
D 018 Citrus (pale green)
E 059 Mallard (teal blue)

hook

US size D-3 (3 mm) crochet hook

gauge

Each hexagon measures 3½ in. (9 cm) edge to edge using a US size D-3 (3 mm) hook.

abbreviations

ch	chain
col	color
cont	continu(e)(ing)
dc	double crochet
MC	main color
rep	repeat
RS	right side
sc	single crochet
sp(s)	space(s)
ss	slip stitch
st(s)	stitch(es)
yoh	yarn over hook

special abbreviations

2dcCL (2-double crochet cluster): [yoh, insert hook in sp, yoh, pull yarn through work, yoh, pull yarn through first 2 loops on hook] twice in same sp (3 loops now on hook), yoh and pull yarn through all 3 loops on hook to complete 2dcCL.

3dcCL (3-double crochet cluster): [yoh, insert hook in sp, yoh, pull yarn through work, yoh, pull yarn through first 2 loops on hook] 3 times in same sp (4 loops now on hook), yoh, pull yarn through all 4 loops on hook to complete the 3dcCL.

color combinations

The blanket is made up of a total of 187 hexagons.

Always using MC for Round 2. One of colors A, B, C, D, or E is used for the center (Round 1) and a different color (A, B, C, D, or E) for Rounds 3 and 4. The following list gives the color combinations and specifies how many hexagons to make in each colorway.

Yellow center (A), off-white (MC), peach (C): 37

Peach center (C), off-white (MC), yellow (A): 38

Pale blue center (B), off-white (MC), teal blue (E): 37

Pale green center (D), off-white (MC), pale blue (B): 38

Teal blue center (E), off-white (MC), pale green (D): 37

Hexagon motif chart

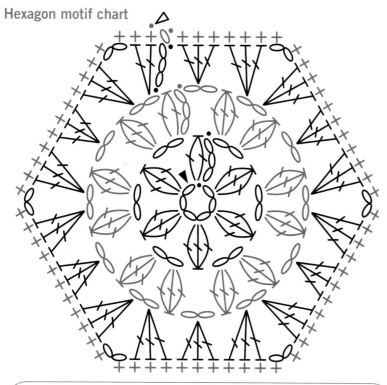

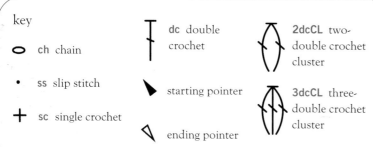

key

○   **ch** chain

•   **ss** slip stitch

✚   **sc** single crochet

⊤   **dc** double crochet

◀   starting pointer

◁   ending pointer

2dcCL two-double crochet cluster

3dcCL three-double crochet cluster

Layout of hexagons

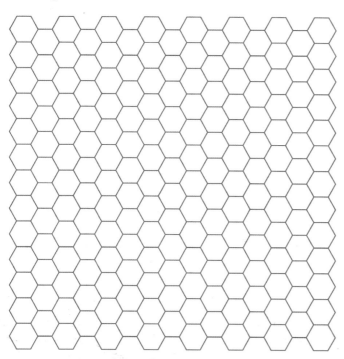

To make the blanket

(make a total of 187 hexagons)

See the Color Combinations on page 85 for which color to use for Round 1 (center) and which color to use for Rounds 3 and 4.

Foundation ring: Using one of col A, B, C, D, or E, make 6ch and join with a ss in first chain to form a ring.

Round 1 (RS): 3ch, 2dcCL in ring, 2ch, [3dcCL in ring, 2ch] 5 times, join with a ss in 3rd of first 3-ch. *6 clusters.* Fasten off.

Cont in rounds with RS always facing you.

Round 2: Join MC (off-white) with a ss in any 2-ch sp between any 3dcCL groups from previous Round, 3ch, [2dcCL, 2ch, 3dcCL] in same ch sp, *2ch, [3dcCL, 2ch, 3dcCL] in next 2-ch sp; rep from * 4 times more, 2ch, join with a ss in 3rd of first 3-ch. *12 clusters.* Fasten off.

Round 3 (hexagon round): Join a contrasting col from A, B, C, D, or E with a ss in 2-ch sp in middle of any "3dcCL, 2ch, 3dcCL" group, 3ch, [2dc, 2ch, 3dc] in same sp (corner), *3dc in next 2-ch sp, [3dc, 2ch, 3dc] in next ch sp (corner); rep from * 4 times more, 3dc in next ch sp, join with a ss in 3rd of first 3-ch. *6 corners.* Do not fasten off.

Round 4: Continue using same col, 1ch, 1sc in each of next 2 sts, 2sc in next ch sp (corner), *1sc in each of next 9 sts, 2sc in next ch sp (corner); rep from * 4 times more, 1sc in each of next 6 sts, join with a ss in top of first sc. Fasten off.

To join the hexagons

Sew in yarn ends, using a yarn sewing needle.

Use MC to join.

Lay hexagons out on a flat surface to evenly arrange the colors. Using the diagram (left) as an example, alternate hexagons in rows of 12 and then 13, starting the first row with 12 hexagons and ending the last row with 12 hexagons.

Using MC, join hexagons with a single crochet seam (See Workshop 3, single crochet seam, page 43) with seam showing on right side.

To make the edging

With RS facing, join MC in top left-hand corner in 2nd of 2 corner sc at top of first hexagon on first row, 1ch, 3sc in same place as join, work 1sc in each sc along each straight edge, 3sc in 2nd of 2 sc at each corner and 1ss in each seam around outer edge, ss in first sc. Fasten off.

Workshop 10

Bobbles

Bobbles are a raised group of stitches created by making a five-double crochet cluster in one stitch. For Blackberry salad stitch, which we use in the Bobble Bag pattern in this Workshop, the bobbles are made with single crochet stitches on either side of the cluster, which makes the bobble stick out to create a more raised texture. At the end of the project are instructions to line the bag with fabric.

Five-double crochet cluster/bobble (5dcCL)

Bobbles are created when working on wrong-side rows and the bobble is pushed out toward the right side row, so begin by working with the wrong side of your work facing you.

1 Yarn over hook and then insert the hook in the stitch, yarn over hook and pull the yarn through the work (3 loops on hook).

2 Yarn over hook and pull the yarn through the first 2 loops on the hook (2 loops left on hook).

3 Yarn over hook, insert the hook in the same stitch, yarn over hook and pull the yarn through the work (4 loops on hook), yarn over hook, pull the yarn through the first 2 loops on the hook (3 loops left on hook).

4 Yarn over hook, insert the hook in the same stitch, yarn over hook and pull the yarn through the work (5 loops on hook), yarn over hook and pull the yarn through the first 2 loops on the hook (4 loops left on hook).

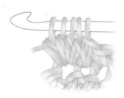

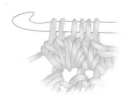

5 Yarn over hook, insert the hook in the same stitch, yarn over hook and pull the yarn through the work (6 loops on hook), yarn over hook and pull the yarn through the first 2 loops on the hook (5 loops left on hook).

6 Yarn over hook, insert the hook in the same stitch, yarn over hook and pull the yarn through the work (7 loops on hook), yarn over hook and pull the yarn through the first 2 loops on the hook (6 loops left on hook).

7 Yarn over hook, pull the yarn through all 6 loops on the hook (1 loop left on hook).

8 Make 1 chain to complete the five-double crochet cluster.

five-double crochet cluster (5dcCL) in symbols

Blackberry salad stitch

This pattern using the 5-double crochet cluster
is called Blackberry salad stitch—this version
is in multiples of four stitches.

Multiples of 4 + 4 stitches.

Foundation chain: Make 8ch.
Row 1 (WS): 1sc in 2nd ch from hook, 1sc in each ch to
end. *11 sc.*
Begin pattern.
Row 2 (WS): 1ch, *1sc in each of first 3 sc, 5dcCL in next
sc, 1sc in each of last 3 sc. *1 bobble.*
Row 3: 1ch, 1sc in each of first 3 sc, 1sc in top of next
5dcCL, 1sc in each of last 3 sc.
Row 4: 1ch, 1sc in first sc, 5dcCL in next sc, 1sc in each of
next 3 sc, 5dcCL in next sc, 1sc in last sc. *2 bobbles.*
Row 5: 1ch, 1sc in first sc, 1sc in top of next 5dcCL, 1sc in
each of next 3 sc, 1sc in top of next 5dcCL, 1sc in last sc.
Rep Rows 2–5 to form pattern.

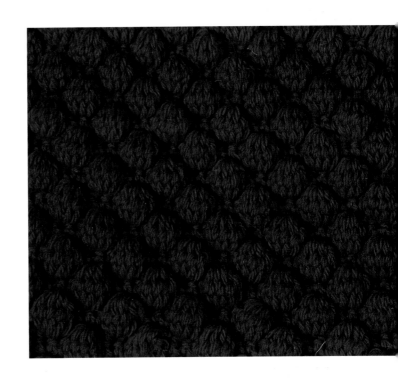

Blackberry salad stitch chart

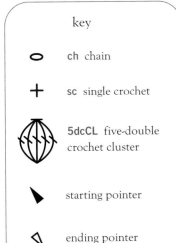

key	
o	**ch** chain
+	**sc** single crochet
⬮	**5dcCL** five-double crochet cluster
▶	starting pointer
▷	ending pointer

Bobble Bag

This fabric-lined bag is great for keeping all your yarn
and crochet equipment in—or simply use it as book
or shopping bag. It features a lovely and very satisfying
bobble stitch.

To make the bag front

Foundation chain: Using MC, make 40ch.
Base row (RS): 1sc in 2nd chain from hook, 1sc in each ch
to end. *39 sc.*
Begin working the bobble pattern as follows:
Row 1 (WS): 1ch, 1sc in first sc, *5dcCL in next sc, 1sc in
each of next 3 sc; rep from * to last 2 sc, 5dcCL in next sc,
1sc in last sc. *10 bobbles.*
Row 2: 1ch, 1sc in first sc, *1sc in top of 5dcCL, 1sc in
each of next 3 sc; rep from * to last 2 sts, 1sc in top of next
5dcCL, 1sc in last sc.

techniques used

Stitches—single crochet, bobble stitch

Making bobbles

Reading a symbol diagram

Adding a 3-round single crochet edging
around the top of a bag

Lining a crocheted bag

Making small pompoms with plaited
hanging tails

bag measurements

Finished bag measures 12 x 15¾ in.
(30 x 40 cm), including edging.

yarns

Bag:
Cascade Yarns *Cascade* 220 (100%
Peruvian Highland wool) Aran- (worsted-)
weight yarn

3 x 3½oz (100g) hanks—approx. 657yd
(600m)—of main color:

MC 9404 Ruby (deep red)

Pompoms:
Scraps of yarn of any weight in four
contrasting colors:

A dark pink
B pale pink
C light green
D light blue

hook

US size H-8 (5 mm) crochet hook

extras

34 x 24 in. (85 x 60 cm) of cotton fabric and
matching sewing thread, for lining

gauge

14 sts x 6 rows over a 4 in. (10 cm) square
worked in double crochet using a US size
H-8 (5 mm) hook and MC.
13 sts x 18 rows over a 4 in. (10 cm) square
worked in bobble pattern using a US size
H-8 (5 mm) hook and MC.

abbreviations

ch	chain
cont	continu(e)(ing)
dc	double crochet
MC	main color
patt(s)	pattern(s)
rep	repeat
RS	right side
sc	single crochet
ss	slip stitch
st(s)	stitch(es)
WS	wrong side
yoh	yarn over hook

special abbreviation

5dcCL (5-double crochet cluster/bobble):
yoh, insert hook in st, yoh and pull yarn
through work (3 loops on hook), yoh, pull
yarn through first 2 loops on hook (2 loops
on hook), [yoh, insert hook in same st, yoh,
pull yarn through work, yoh, pull yarn
through first 2 loops on hook] 4 times (6
loops on hook), yoh and pull yarn through all
6 loops on hook, then make 1 ch to
complete the 5dcCL.

notes

The bobbles (5dcCLs) are made on
wrong-side rows, so make sure they are
pushed toward the right side as you
make them.

Row 3: 1ch, 1sc in each of first 3 sc, *5dcCL in next sc, 1sc in each of next 3 sc; rep from * to end. *9 bobbles.*
Row 4: 1ch, 1sc in each of first 3 sc, *1sc in top of next 5dcCL, 1sc in each of next 3 sc; rep from * to end.
Rep Rows 1–4 to form bobble pattern.
Cont in patt until work measures 15 in. (38 cm), ending on a patt Row 2.
Fasten off.

To make the bag back
Make exactly as for the bag front.

To make the handles
(Make two)
Foundation chain: Using MC, make 8ch.
Row 1 (WS): 1sc in 2nd ch from hook, 1sc in each ch to end. *7 sc.*
Row 2 (RS): 1ch, 1sc in each sc to end.
Rep Row 2 twice more, so ending on a RS row.

key

o   **ch** chain

+   **sc** single crochet

5dcCL five-double
crochet cluster

▶   starting pointer

◁   ending pointer

Blackberry salad stitch chart

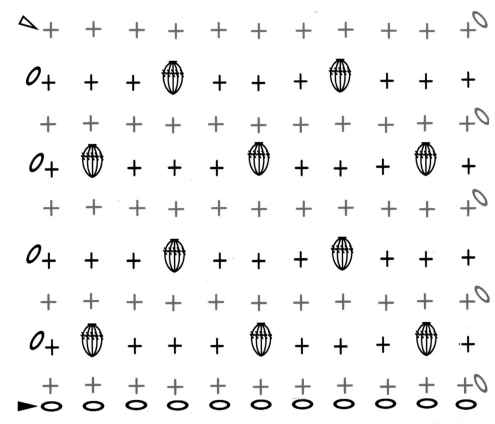

Begin working the bobble pattern as follows:

Row 1 (WS): 1ch, *1sc in each of first 3 sc, 5dcCL in next sc, 1sc in each of last 3 sc. *1 bobble.*

Row 2: 1ch, 1sc in each of first 3 sc, 1sc in top of next 5dcCL, 1sc in each of last 3 sc.

Row 3: 1ch, 1sc in first sc, 5dcCL in next sc, 1sc in each of next 3 sc, 5dcCL in next sc, 1sc in last sc. *2 bobbles.*

Row 4: 1ch, 1sc in first sc, 1sc in top of next 5dcCL, 1sc in each of next 3 sc, 1sc in top of next 5dcCL, 1sc in last sc.

Rep Rows 1–4 to form bobble pattern.

Cont in pattern until handle measures 20¼ in. (51.5 cm) from foundation-ch edge, ending on a Row 2.

Next row: 1ch, 1sc in each sc to end.

Rep last row 3 times more.

Fasten off.

To work the double-crochet edging

Using a yarn sewing needle and MC, and with the right sides of the bag front and back together, join side and bottom seams, leaving top open. Sew in all yarn ends. Turn the bag right side out.

Using MC and hook, work the edging around the top edge of the bag as follows:

Round 1 (RS): With RS facing, join yarn with a ss to top

edge at one seam, 1ch, 1sc in same place as ss, 1sc in each sc to end.

Cont in rounds in a spiral with RS always facing you and marking beginning of each round.

Round 2: 1sc in each sc to end.

Rep last round once more, join with a ss to next sc.

Fasten off.

To finish the bag

Line the crochet bag with fabric lining (see page 94). Make two small pompoms in each in A, B, C, and D (see pages 64–65). When tying each pompom, leave the two yarn tails at least 12 in. (30 cm) long. Thread one more strand of yarn through each pompom so there are now three long yarn tails. Braid the three yarn tails together on each pompom and knot the end.

Tie all the pompoms braids together in a bunch so they hang down at different lengths, and trim off the ends near the final knot.

Make a separate 10 in. (25 cm) braid with one of the pompom colors and use it to tie the bunch of pompoms to the bottom of one handle, so they drape down one side of the bag.

Fabric lining for crochet bags

It's not necessary to line crochet bags, but it helps if you do. Yarn is a stretchy fabric and adding a fabric lining will strengthen the bag and hold it in shape. However, you do need some basic sewing skills to be able to achieve this.

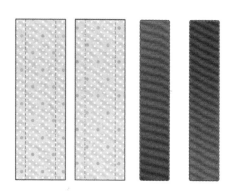

1 Measure the crochet straps and cut out the handle lining the same size as plus an extra ⅝ in. (1.5 cm) on each side for the hem.

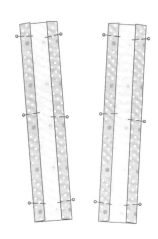

2 Press a ⅝ in. (1.5 cm) wide hem to the wrong side along each long edge of the fabric strips and pin in place.

3 Place the lining with the hem side down onto the wrong side of the crocheted handle. Pin and then hand sew the lining to the crocheted handle using a simple whip stitch. Rep for the second handle. Remove the pins.

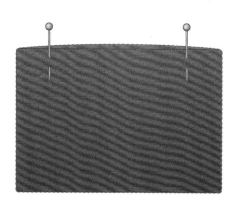

4 Place a pin marker 1 in. (2.5 cm) in from each outside seam along the top edge of the crocheted bag, on both the front and the back.

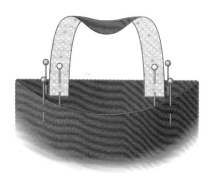

5 With the crocheted side of the handle to the inside of the bag, attach the ends of the first handle so they extend down into the bag by about 2 in. (5 cm), with the outer edge of each handle to a pin marker. Pin in place and then hand sew the handle to the bag. Repeat on the other side of the bag to add the other handle and then remove any remaining pins.

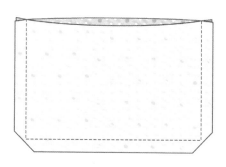

6 Cut two pieces of lining fabric to the same size as the bag plus an extra ⅝ in. (1.5 cm) allowance for seams on the sides and bottom and an extra 1 in. (2.5 cm) at the top. Pin the fabric pieces right sides together and machine sew the side and bottom seams. Trim across the bottom corners and press out seams.

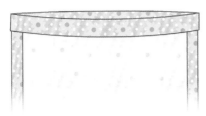

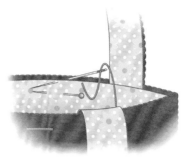

7 Turn the top edge of the lining over to the wrong side by 1 in. (2.5 cm) and press.

8 Insert the lining into the bag with wrong sides of crochet and lining together and pin in place around the top edge. Hand sew the lining to the crocheted piece around the top edge, stitching across the handles again for extra security.

Workshop 11

Working with lace yarn, fans, and picots

Lace is a fine yarn and even if you are crocheting on a large hook it is slow to work with. It can give a wonderful lacy effect though—for the project in this Workshop I've designed a beautiful Lace Scarf, which also includes fans, V stitches, and a delicate picot edging.

Lace weight yarn

Lace is a fine yarn that usually comes on hanks and needs to be wound into a ball before you can use it, which takes a lot of time. If you are only crocheting in the evenings, allow the first evening for manually winding the ball(s). Lace is light in weight and so there will be a lot of "length" on the hank. Also give yourself more time for

making the projects because fine yarn will be slower to work with.

Lace can be worked on all different sizes of crochet hooks; the smaller the hook, the tighter the fabric. For the project in this workshop I have used a US size H-8 (5mm) hook that when used with lace gives a more open and "lacy" effect.

Fans

Fans are groups of stitches worked into the same stitch to create a V-shape fan-like effect. In the Lace Scarf project with this Workshop, the fan group worked is 3 double crochet, 1 chain, 3 double crochet (3dc, 1ch, 3dc) all worked into the same place.

 fan (fan) in symbols

V stitch (V-st)

V stitches are also groups of stitches that resemble a V shape but they have fewer stitches than fans. V stitches can have different combinations of stitches, but they are usually one stitch followed by a chain and a repeat of the first stitch on the other side of the chain. In the Lace Scarf project with this Workshop the V stitch is 1 half double crochet, 1 chain, 1 half double crochet (1hdc, 1ch, 1hdc) all worked into the same place.

 V stitch (V-st) in symbols

Lace pattern

This lace pattern forms the main design of the scarf, which is the project for this Workshop. Practice it here first.

Multiples of 11 + 1 stitch.

Foundation chain: Make 82ch.
Row 1 (RS): 1sc in 2nd ch from hook, 1sc in next ch, *skip 3 ch, work 1 Fan in next ch, skip 3 ch, 1sc in next ch**, 1ch, skip 1 ch, 1sc in next ch; rep from * ending last rep at **, 1sc in last ch, turn.
Row 2: 2ch (counts as first hdc), 1dc in first sc, *2ch, 1sc in 1-ch sp at center of next Fan, 2ch**, work 1 V-st in 1-ch sp between next 2 sc; rep from * ending last rep at **, skip next sc, 2hdc in last sc.
Row 3: 3ch (counts as first dc), 3dc in first hdc, *1sc in next 2-ch sp, 1ch, 1sc in next 2-ch sp**, work 1 Fan in 1-ch sp at center of next V-st; rep from * ending last rep at **, 4dc in top of 2-ch at end of row.
Row 4: 1ch, 1sc in first dc, *2ch, work 1 V-st in next 1-ch sp between next 2 sc, 2ch**, 1sc in 1-ch sp at center of next Fan; rep from * ending last rep at **, 1sc in top of 3-ch at end of row.
Row 5: 1ch, 1sc in first sc, *1sc in next 2-ch sp, work 1 Fan in 1-ch sp at center of next V-st, 1sc in next 2-ch sp**, 1ch; rep from * ending last rep at **, 1sc in last sc.
Rep Rows 2–5 to form lace pattern.

Lace pattern chart

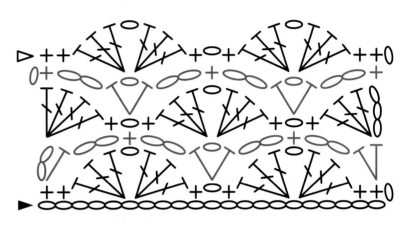

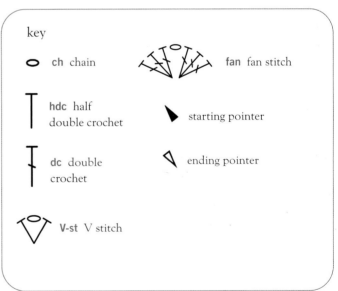

key

○ **ch** chain

⊤ **hdc** half double crochet

†† **dc** double crochet

∨ **V-st** V stitch

fan fan stitch

◤ starting pointer

◁ ending pointer

Picot

A picot is a little bobble texture that is often used to create little points along the outer edge of an edging.

Three-chain picot (3-ch picot) edging

Try making this sample to practice a 3-ch picot edging.

 three-chain picot
(3-ch picot) in symbols

Make 14ch.

Row 1: 1sc in second ch from hook, 1sc in each ch to end.

Row 2: 1ch, 1sc in each of next 2 sts, 3dc in next st, *1sc in each of the next 3 sts, 3dc in next st: rep from * twice more, 2sc in each of last 2 sts.

Row 3 (picot row): 1ch, 1sc in each of next 2sc, 1sc in top of next dc, *3ch.

Ss in third ch from hook (one picot made). 1sc in top of next dc.

Rep from * once more, 3ch, ss in third ch from hook (picot made)**, 1sc in each of next 3sc, 1sc in top of next dc; rep from * ending last rep at **, 1sc in each of last two sc.

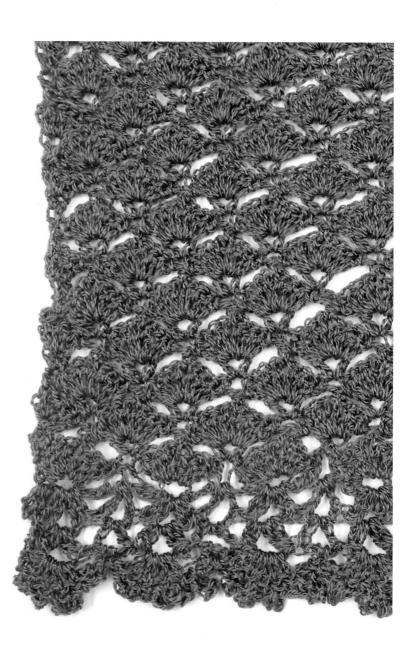

Lace Scarf

I'm a big fan of light scarves and this scarf is beautifully light and pretty. The yarn is a mix of silk and merino and the stitch light and textured.

To make the scarf

Foundation chain: Make 82ch.

Row 1 (RS): 1sc in 2nd ch from hook, 1sc in next ch, *skip 3 ch, work 1 Fan in next ch, skip 3 ch, 1sc in next ch**, 1ch, skip 1 ch, 1sc in next ch; rep from * ending last rep at **, 1sc in last ch, turn.

Row 2: 2ch (counts as first hdc), 1hdc in first sc, *2ch, 1sc in 1-ch sp at center of next Fan, 2ch**, work 1 V-st in 1-ch sp between next 2 sc; rep from * ending last rep at **, skip next sc, 2hdc in last sc.

techniques used

Stitches—double crochet, single crochet, half double crochet

Working with lace yarn

Working textured lace stitches

Working a 3-ch picot shell edging

scarf measurements

Finished scarf measures 10½ x 52½ in. (26.5 x 133 cm).

yarns

Fyberspates *Scrumptious Lace* (55% merino wool, 45% silk) hand-dyed lace-weight yarn

1 x 3½oz (100g) hank—approx. 1094yd 1000m)—of 507 Teal (blue)

hook

US size H-8 (5 mm) crochet hook

gauge

18 sts x 10 rows over a 4 in. (10 cm) square worked in double crochet using a US size H-8 (5 mm) hook.

3 Fans x 10 rows over a 4 in. (10 cm) square worked in Fan and V-st pattern using a US size H-8 (5 mm) hook.

abbreviations

beg	begin(ning)
ch	chain
cont	continu(e)(ing)
dc	double crochet
hdc	half double crochet
rep	repeat
RS	right side
sc	single crochet
sp(s)	space(s)
ss	slip stitch
st(s)	stitch(es)
yoh	yarn over hook

special abbreviations

Fan: Work [3dc, 1ch, 3dc] all in the same place.

V-st: Work [1hdc, 1ch, 1hdc] all in the same place.

2dcCL (2-double crochet cluster): [yoh, insert hook in sp, yoh, pull yarn through work, yoh, pull yarn through first 2 loops on hook] twice in same sp (3 loops now on hook), yoh and pull yarn through all 3 loops on hook to complete 2dcCL.

Row 3: 3ch (counts as first dc), 3dc in first hdc, *1sc in next 2-ch sp, 1ch, 1sc in next 2-ch sp**, work 1 Fan in 1-ch sp at center of next V-st; rep from * ending last rep at **, 4dc in top of 2-ch at end of row.

Row 4: 1ch, 1sc in first dc, *2ch, work 1 V-st in next 1-ch sp between next 2 sc, 2ch**, 1sc in 1-ch sp at center of next Fan; rep from * ending last rep at **, 1sc in top of 3-ch at end of row.

Row 5: 1ch, 1sc in first sc, *1sc in next 2-ch sp, work 1 Fan in 1-ch sp at center of next V-st, 1sc in next 2-ch sp **, 1ch; rep from * ending last rep at **, 1sc in last sc.

Rep Rows 2–5 until scarf measures 48½ in. 123 cm), ending on a Row 2 (which is a WS row).

Do not fasten off, but work top edging along this last row as explained.

Scarf chart

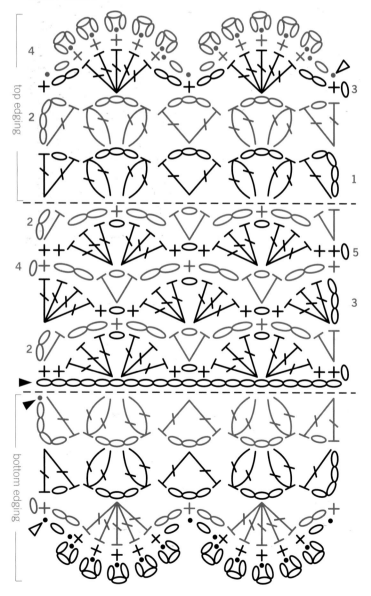

To work the top edging

With RS facing, beg picot-shell edging across last row of scarf as follows:

Row 1 (RS): 4ch (counts as first dc and 1-ch sp), 1dc in first hdc, *[2dcCL, 3ch, 2dcCL] in next sc (at center of Fan)**, [1dc, 3ch, 1dc] in 1-ch sp at center of next V-st; rep from * ending last rep at **, [1dc, 1ch, 1dc] in 2-ch at end of row.

Row 2: 4ch, 1dc in first dc, *[2dcCL, 3ch, 2dcCL] in 3-ch sp at center of next 2 clusters**, [1dc, 3ch, 1dc] in next 3-ch sp at center of next "1dc, 3ch, 1dc" group; rep from * ending last rep at **, [1dc, 1ch, 1dc] in 4-ch sp at end of row.

Row 3: 1ch, 1sc in first dc, 2ch, *5dc in next 3-ch sp (between clusters), 2ch**, 1sc in next 3-ch sp (between doubles), 2ch; rep from * ending last rep at **, 1sc in 4-ch sp at end of row.

Row 4 (picot row): 1ss in first sc, *1ch, [1sc in next dc, for a picot make 3ch, then work 1ss in first of 3-ch just made to complete the picot] 5 times, 1ss in same place as last sc was worked, 1ch, 1ss in next sc; rep from * to end of row. Fasten off.

To work the bottom edging

Work the other edging along the underside of the foundation chain at the other end of the scarf.

With RS facing, join with a ss in first ch of foundation chain and work picot-shell edging as follows:

Row 1 (RS): 4ch (counts as first dc and 1-ch sp), 1dc in same foundation ch, *[2dcCL, 3ch, 2dcCL] in center of bottom of next Fan**, [1dc, 3ch, 1dc] in next 1-ch sp (between 2 sc in Row 1 of scarf); rep from * ending last rep at **, [1dc, 1ch, 1dc] in last foundation ch.

Rows 2–4: Work as for Rows 2–4 of top edging. Fasten off.

To finish the scarf

Using a yarn sewing needle, sew in the yarn ends. Do not press.

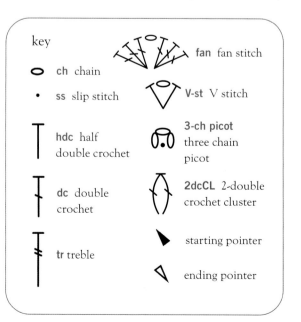

Workshop 12

Fans and Clusters

Fans and clusters make up some very interesting shapes in crochet and one of my favorite patterns is Catherine Wheel Stitch, which is made by making 7-double crochet fans over the top of 7-double crochet clusters. The project for this Workshop is a really super soft Catherine Wheel Stitch Blanket made using a chunky yarn, so it grows very quickly.

Working with charts

If you haven't attempted any of the charts yet in this book, then now is the time to start. Catherine Wheel stitch is made up of doubles and clusters, but the secret is in where to put them and seeing them placed in the chart helps you understand the shape of this stitch a lot.

You don't have to use the same yarn as in this project. This stitch works really well with finer yarns and cottons too. You can also make a Catherine Wheel stitch using 2-row stripes—use color A for the first row and then change to the next color for the next two rows, then continue by changing color every two rows. When working with a lot of stitches across one row, it's important to have the correct number of stitches in the foundation chain. I usually count in 20s or 50s and add a little stitch marker each time to make counting back my stitches easier. Make sure when making the foundation chain that you have no distractions to make you lose count.

When working with a lot of loops on your hook, as with the 7-double crochet cluster in this pattern, it's also important to keep your work loose. If the loops are too tight on the crochet hook, you won't be able to pull the yarn through all the loops.

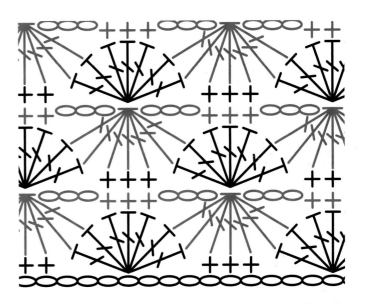

TIP
It's very easy to forget how many stitches you've worked, so it's important to keep going back and having a quick glance at the end of each row. If you have too few doubles in the fans or clusters, it will throw out the pattern on the following row.

Seven-double crochet cluster (7dcCL)

   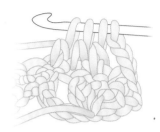

1 Yarn over hook, insert the hook in the next stitch, yarn over hook, pull the yarn through the work (3 loops on hook).

2 Yarn over hook, pull the yarn through the first 2 loops on the hook (2 loops on hook).

3 Yarn over hook, insert the hook in the next stitch, yarn over hook, pull the yarn through the work (4 loops on hook), yarn over hook, pull the yarn through the first 2 loops on the hook (3 loops on hook).

4 Yarn over hook, insert the hook in the next stitch, yarn over hook, pull the yarn through the work (5 loops on hook), yarn over hook, pull the yarn through the first 2 loops on the hook (4 loops on hook).

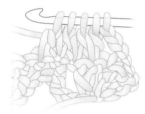 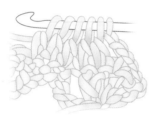 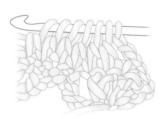 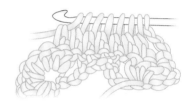

5 Yarn over hook, insert the hook in the next stitch, yarn over hook, pull the yarn through the work (6 loops on hook), yarn over hook, pull the yarn through the first 2 loops on the hook (5 loops on hook).

6 Yarn over hook, insert the hook in the next stitch, yarn over hook, pull the yarn through the work (7 loops on hook), yarn over hook, pull the yarn through the first 2 loops on the hook (6 loops on hook).

7 Yarn over hook, insert the hook in the next stitch, yarn over hook, pull the yarn through the work (8 loops on hook), yarn over hook, pull the yarn through the first 2 loops on the hook (7 loops on hook).

8 Yarn over hook, insert the hook in the next st, yarn over hook, pull the yarn through the work (9 loops on hook), yarn over hook, pull the yarn through the first 2 loops on the hook (8 loops on hook).

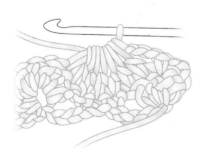

9 Yarn over hook, pull the yarn through all 8 loops on the hook (1 loop on hook). One 7-double crochet cluster made.

seven-double crochet cluster (7dcCL) in symbols

Catherine wheel stitch

Catherine Wheel Stitch is made by making 7-double crochet fans over the top of 7-double crochet clusters. If you want to make it in stripes, change to the second color in Row 2 and work two rows in each color from there on.

Multiples of 10 + 7 stitches.

Foundation chain: Using MC, make 37ch.
Row 1 (RS): 1sc in 2nd ch from hook, 1sc in next ch, *skip 3 ch, 7dc in next ch, skip 3 ch, 1sc in each of next 3 ch; rep from * to last 4 ch, skip 3 ch, 4dc in last ch.
Row 2 (WS): 1ch, 1sc in each of first 2 dc, *3ch, 7dcCL over next 7 sts, 3ch, 1sc in each of next 3 sts; rep from * to last 4 sts, 3ch, 4dcCL over last 4 sts.
Row 3: 3ch (counts as 1 dc), 3dc in top of 4dcCL, *skip 3 ch, 1sc in each of next 3 sc, skip 3 ch, 7dc in top of next 7dcCL; rep from * to end, ending with skip 3 ch, 1sc in each of last 2 sc.
Row 4: 3ch (counts as 1 dc), skip first st, 3dcCL over next 3 sts, *3ch, 1sc in each of next 3 sts, 3ch, 7dcCL over next 7 sts; rep from * to end, ending with 3ch, 1sc in next st, 1sc in 3rd of 3-ch from previous row.
Row 5: 1ch, 1sc in each of first 2 sc, *skip 3 ch, 7dc in top of next 7dcCL, skip 3 ch, 1sc in each of next 3 sc; rep from * to end, ending skip 3 ch, 4dc in 3rd of 3-ch from previous row.
Rep Rows 2–5 to form pattern.

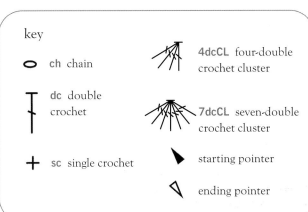

key

○ **ch** chain

| **dc** double crochet

+ **sc** single crochet

4dcCL four-double crochet cluster

7dcCL seven-double crochet cluster

▶ starting pointer

▷ ending pointer

Catherine wheel stitch chart

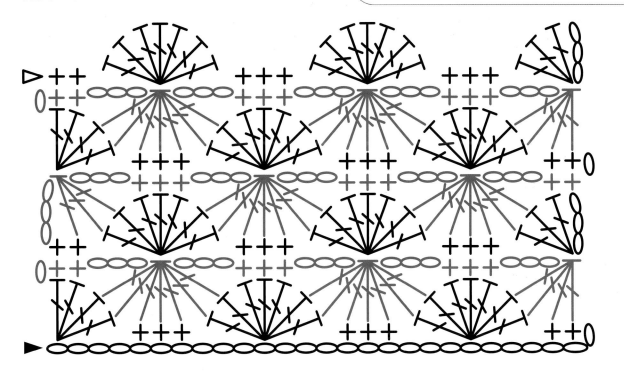

Catherine Wheel Stitch Blanket

This blanket is made using a chunky alpaca/merino mix of wool, which is a luxurious wool, but can be made in any type of yarn. Use a multiple of 10 stitches plus 7 stitches in the pattern if you want to change the width.

techniques used

Stitches—single crochet, double crochet

Working Catherine Wheel Stitch

Making clusters

blanket measurements

Finished blanket measures approximately 49¼ x 55½ in. 125 x 141 cm).

yarns

Debbie Bliss *Paloma* (60% alpaca, 40% wool) super-chunky- (super-bulky-) weight yarn

24 x 1¾oz (50g) hanks—approx. 1704yd (1560m)—of main color:

MC 18 Light Pink (pale pink)

4 x 1¾oz (50g) hanks—approx. 284yd (260m)—of a contrasting color for edging:

A 19 Dusky Rose (mid pink)

hook

US size L-11 (7 mm) crochet hook

gauge

10 sts (1 pattern repeat) measure 3¼ in. (8.5 cm) and 4 rows (1 pattern repeat) measure 3 in. (7.5 cm) using a US size L-11 (7 mm) hook.

abbreviations

ch	chain
dc	double crochet
MC	main color
rep	repeat
RS	right side
sc	single crochet
ss	slip stitch
st(s)	stitch(es)
WS	wrong side
yoh	yarn over hook

special abbreviations

7dcCL (7-double crochet cluster): [yoh, insert hook in next st, yoh, pull yarn through work, yoh, pull yarn through first 2 loops on hook] 7 times in same st (8 loops now on hook), yoh, pull yarn through all 8 loops on hook to complete the 7dcCL.

4dcCL (4-double crochet cluster): [yoh, insert hook in next st, yoh, pull yarn through work, yoh, pull yarn through first 2 loops on hook] 4 times in same st (5 loops now on hook), yoh, pull yarn through all 5 loops on hook to complete the 4dcCL.

3dcCL (3-double crochet cluster): [yoh, insert hook in next st, yoh, pull yarn through work, yoh, pull yarn through first 2 loops on hook] 3 times in same st (4 loops now on hook), yoh, pull yarn through all 4 loops on hook to complete the 3dcCL.

Catherine wheel stitch chart

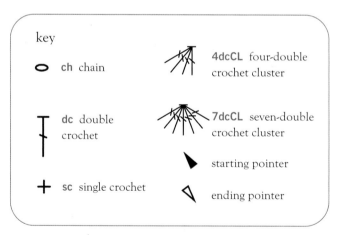

To make the blanket

Foundation chain: Using MC, make 137ch.

Row 1 (RS): 1sc in 2nd ch from hook, 1sc in next ch, *skip 3 ch, 7dc in next ch, skip 3 ch, 1sc in each of next 3 ch; rep from * to last 4 ch, skip 3 ch, 4dc in last ch.

Row 2 (WS): 1ch, 1sc in each of first 2 dc, *3ch, 7dcCL over next 7 sts, 3ch, 1sc in each of next 3 sts; rep from * to last 4 sts, 3ch, 4dcCL over last 4 sts.

Row 3: 3ch (counts as 1dc), 3dc in top of 4dcCL, *skip 3 ch, 1sc in each of next 3 sc, skip 3 ch, 7dc in top of next 7dcCL; rep from * to end, ending with skip 3 ch, 1sc in each of last 2 sc.

Row 4: 3ch (counts as 1dc), skip first st, 3dcCL over next 3 sts, *3ch, 1sc in each of next 3 sts, 3ch, 7dcCL over next 7 sts; rep from * to end, ending with 3ch, 1sc in next st, 1sc in 3rd of 3-ch from previous row.

Row 5: 1ch, 1sc in each of first 2 sc, *skip 3 ch, 7dc in top of next 7dcCL, skip 3 ch, 1sc in each of next 3 sc; rep from * to end, ending skip 3 ch, 4dc in 3rd of 3-ch from previous row.

Rep Rows 2–5 until work measures approx. 51½ in. (131 cm), ending on a Row 2.

Fasten off.

Sew in yarn ends, using a yarn sewing needle.

key

○ **ch** chain

⊤ **dc** double crochet

✚ **sc** single crochet

4dcCL four-double crochet cluster

7dcCL seven-double crochet cluster

▶ starting pointer

◁ ending pointer

Edging

Round 1: With RS facing, join A with a ss in one of the corner stitches, 1ch, 2sc in same st, sc evenly along each side of blanket into sts and spaces, making 3sc in each corner st, join with a ss in first sc.

Round 2: 1ch, 1sc in each st around each side, making 3sc into center st at each corner, join with a ss in first sc.

Rep Round 2 three times more.

Fasten off.

Sew in ends.

Workshop 13

Working with cotton

Cotton yarn was once popular for crocheting very fine doilies and seat back covers but is no longer used so much, although the thicker cottons now available are perfect for summer garments and accessories. For this Workshop I created a pretty Shelf Edging in light worsted (double knit/DK) cotton yarn, which is great for practicing clusters and picots and is decorated with the Daisy learned in Workshop 5. I've also included a crochet Rose for you to try and a new stitch, treble crochet.

Working with cotton

Cotton yarn used to be the preferred choice in the early 20th century, but since new softer yarns were introduced crocheting with cotton is less common. Cotton yarns tend to have less stretch than other yarns so can be firmer to work with. They come in all thicknesses and can be mixed with other fibers to create a softer texture. Cotton is easy to wash—you can just throw it in the washing machine.

Edging

This pretty edging can be used on many of your crochet projects. Try it a few times until you are confident and then put it into practice in the Shelf Edging project.

Multiples of 12 + 4 stitches.

Foundation chain: Using MC (red), make 160 ch.
Row 1 (RS): 1sc in 4th ch from hook, *5ch, skip 3 ch, 1sc in next ch; rep from * to end.
Row 2: 2ch, 1sc in first 5-ch sp, [2dcCL, 2ch, 1sc, 5ch, 1sc, 2ch, 2dcCL] all in next 5-ch sp, *1sc in next 5-ch sp, 5ch, 1sc in next ch sp, [2dcCL, 2ch, 1sc, 5ch, 1sc, 2ch, 2dcCL] all in next 5-ch sp; rep from * to last 5-ch sp, ending 1sc in last 5-ch sp, 5ch, 1sc in 3-ch sp at end of row.

Row 3: 1sc in first 5-ch sp, 5ch, [3dcCL, 4ch, 3dcCL] all in next 5-ch sp (between 2dcCL groups), *5ch, 1sc in next 5-ch sp (between 2 sc), 5ch, [3dcCL, 4ch, 3dcCL] all in next 5-ch sp (between 2dcCL groups); rep from * ending 5ch, 1sc in 2-ch sp at end of row.
Row 4: *3sc in next ch sp, [3ch, 1ss in 3rd ch from hook (picot made), 2sc in same ch sp; rep from * in each ch sp to end, ending with 1ss in sc at end of row.
Fasten off.

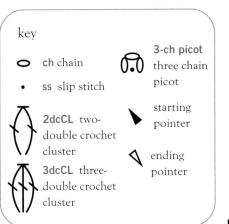

key

○ ch chain

• ss slip stitch

2dcCL two-double crochet cluster

3dcCL three-double crochet cluster

3-ch picot three chain picot

▶ starting pointer

▽ ending pointer

Edging chart

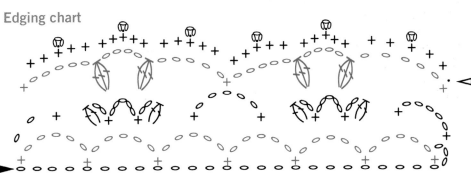

Flowers

The flowers for the Shelf Edging really need to have flat petals; if you don't want to use the Daisy on page 57, try the 5-petal flower on page 44. A flatter flower will sit better when attached to a border—if you use 3-D flowers, the weight and shape can make them droop when attached to garlands. However, the roses below are really pretty embellishments for other projects and can be made in any thickness or yarn.

Roses

Make these to decorate hats, scarves or cushions—or give a jar full of them as a gift.

Using US size G/6 (4 mm) hook, make 53ch. Work all petals along 53ch with RS facing as follows.

Petal 1: 1dc in 3rd ch from hook, 1dc in each of next 2 ch, 3ch, 1ss in next ch.
Petal 2: 4ch, 1tr in each of next 3 ch, 3ch, 1ss in next ch.
Petal 3: 4ch, 1tr in each of next 4 ch, 3ch, 1ss in next ch.
Petal 4: 4ch, 1tr in each of next 5 ch, 3ch, 1ss in next ch.

Petal 5: 4ch, 1tr in each of next 6 ch, 3ch, 1ss in next ch.
Petal 6: 3ch, 1dc in each of next 2 ch, 3ch, 1ss in next ch.
Petal 7: 4ch, 1tr in each of next 3 ch, 3ch, 1ss in next ch.
Petal 8: 4ch, 1tr in each of next 4 ch, 3ch, 1ss in next ch.
Petal 9: 4ch, 1tr in each of next 5 ch, 3ch, 1ss in next ch.
Petal 10: 4ch, 1tr in each of next 6 ch, 3ch, 1ss in last ch.
Fasten off.

Rose chart

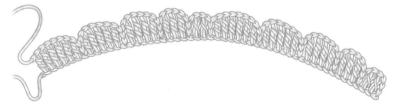

1 The strip of crochet you have made has small and large scallops along one edge, which will become the petals of the rose.

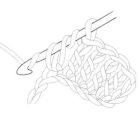

2 To make up roses, with WS facing and starting with first petal (smallest), coil the petal strip up keeping the base flat at the chain edge as shown left. Insert a large glass-headed pin across the base of the rose to hold it in position. Stitch the petals in place across the base using a yarn sewing needle and matching yarn.

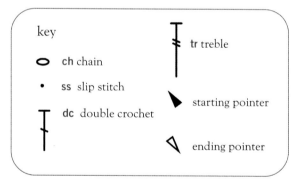

key

○ **ch** chain

• **ss** slip stitch

⊤ **dc** double crochet

⊤ (with marks) **tr** treble

▶ starting pointer

◁ ending pointer

3 From the front, the curves at the top edge create the effect of the petals of the rose.

Treble (tr)

This stitch is longer than double and requires more wraps of the yarn. It creates a very open fabric.

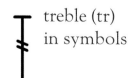

Yarn over hook twice, insert the hook in the stitch or chain, yarn over hook, pull the yarn through the work (4 loops on hook), [yarn over hook, pull yarn through first two loops on the hook] twice (2 loops on hook), yarn over hook, pull yarn through last two loops (1 loop on hook).

⊤ treble (tr) in symbols

Shelf Edging

Brighten up drab old shelves with
this lovely edging. I always think
that a bit of textile looks really well
against wood and makes dressers
and shelves look interesting.

To change the length of your edging

The instructions are for an edging that is 32 in. (81 cm)
long, with a daisy at each end and with five daisies
evenly spaced between—a total of seven daisies.
It is easy to alter the length of the edging. The edging
is worked over a multiple of 12 foundation chains, plus
4 foundation chain extra. Each length of 12 foundation
chains makes a 2½ in. (6.25 cm) length of edging. So
that the edging begins and ends with a flower, you need
to make an odd number of 12-ch sections.

techniques used

Stitches—single crochet, double
crochet, half double crochet

Making two-double and three-double
crochet clusters

Creating a decorative crochet edging

Making 11-petal daisies

How to use crochet edgings

edging measurements

Finished edging is approximately 6 in.
(15 cm) deep, including the daisies.
The edging given in the instructions is
approximately 32 in. (81 cm) long, but
the length is adjustable.

yarns

Rowan *Cotton Glacé* (100% cotton)
lightweight (light worsted) yarn

1 x 1¾oz (50g) ball—approx. 125yd
(115m)—of each of four colors:

MC 741 Poppy (red)
A 849 Winsor (blue-green)
B 856 Mineral (golden yellow)
C 725 Ecru (off-white)

hook

US size D-3 (3 mm) crochet hook

gauge

Shelf edging measures 2¾ in. (7 cm)
deep (without the flowers) and each
shelf edging repeat (lengthwise along
edging—worked over 12 foundation
chains) measures 5 in. (12.5 cm) using
a US size D-3 (3 mm) hook.
Flower motif measures 3 in. (7.5 cm) in
diameter using a US size D-3 (3 mm)
crochet hook.

abbreviations

ch	chain
dc	double crochet
rep	repeat
RS	right side
sc	single crochet
sp(s)	space(s)
ss	slip stitch
st(s)	stitch(es)
yoh	yarn over hook

special abbreviations

2dcCL (two-double crochet cluster):
[yoh, insert hook in sp (or st), yoh, pull
yarn through work, yoh, pull yarn
through first 2 loops on hook] twice in
same sp/st (3 loops now on hook), yoh
and pull yarn through all 3 loops on hook
to complete 2dcCL.

3dcCL (three-double crochet cluster):
[yoh, insert hook in sp (or st), yoh, pull
yarn through work, yoh, pull yarn
through first 2 loops on hook] 3 times in
same sp/st (4 loops now on hook), yoh,
pull yarn through all 4 loops on hook to
complete the 3dcCL.

The edging in the instructions has thirteen 12-ch sections. You can make the edging longer (or shorter) in 5 in. (12.5 cm) sections by adding (or subtracting) 24 foundation chains. For each extra 24-ch section you will need one more flower (or one fewer flowers if you are reducing the length). For example, for an edging 37 in. (93.5 cm) long and with eight flowers, start with 184 foundation chains; for an edging 42 in. (106 cm) long and with nine flowers, start with 208 foundation chains; and so on. For a shorter edging that is 27 in. (68.5 cm) long and has six flowers, start with 136 foundation chains; for an edging that is 22 in. (56 cm) long and has five flowers, start with 112 foundation chains; and so on.

To make the bottom of the edging

The foundation chain will be at the top of the edging and Row 4 will be at the bottom of the edging.

Foundation chain: Using MC, make 160ch.

Row 1 (RS): 1sc in 4th ch from hook, *5ch, skip 3 ch, 1sc in next ch; rep from * to end.

Row 2: 2ch, 1sc in first 5-ch sp, [2dcCL, 2ch, 1sc, 5ch, 1sc, 2ch, 2dcCL] all in next 5-ch sp, *1sc in next 5-ch sp, 5ch, 1sc in next ch sp, [2dcCL, 2ch, 1sc, 5ch, 1sc, 2ch, 2dcCL] all in next 5-ch sp; rep from * to last 5-ch sp, ending 1sc in last 5-ch sp, 5ch, 1sc in 3-ch sp at end of row.

Row 3: 1sc in first 5-ch sp, 5ch, [3dcCL, 4ch, 3dcCL] all in next 5-ch sp (between 2dcCL groups), *5ch, 1sc in next 5-ch sp (between 2 sc) , 5ch, [3dcCL, 4ch, 3dcCL] all in next 5-ch sp (between 2dcCL groups); rep from * ending 5ch, 1sc in 2-ch sp at end of row.

Row 4: *3sc in next ch sp, [3ch, 1ss in 3rd ch from hook (picot made)], 2sc in same ch sp; rep from * in each ch sp to end, ending with 1ss in sc at end of row.

Fasten off.

To make the top of the edging

With the foundation chain uppermost, RS of edging facing and using A, join yarn with a ss to first foundation chain, 6ch, 1ss in 3rd ch from hook (picot made), *3ch, skip 3 foundation ch, 1dc in next ch (in underside of same ch next sc is worked), 3ch, 1ss in top of dc (picot made); rep from * to end of foundation chain.

Fasten off.

To make the daisy

(Make 7 daisies)

Note: If you are making a longer or shorter edging, refer to the instructions for varying the length of the edging and make as many daisies as required.

Foundation ring: Using B, make 6ch and join with a ss in first ch to form a ring.

Round 1 (RS): 1ch (counts as 1sc), 10sc in ring, join with a ss in first ch. *11 sts.*

Fasten off A.

Round 2 (RS): With RS facing, using C and working in front loop only of sc, join yarn with a ss in front loop of any st in Round 1, *6ch, 1hdc in 3rd ch from hook, 1dc in each of next 2 ch, 1sc in next ch, 1ss in same front loop as last ss was worked, 1ss in front loop of next sc of Round 1; rep from *, ending with 1ss in same front loop as first ss of round.

Fasten off.

To finish the edging

Using a yarn sewing needle, sew in all yarn ends on the daisies and the edging.

Block and press the flowers with a damp cloth.

Each flower is positioned over 3 picots along the bottom of the edging—with a 3dcCL at the center of these 3 picots—and there are 3 picots free between the flowers. Mark the positions for the flowers. To join on the first flower, hold the edging with RS facing and with the bottom edge uppermost. Using A, join yarn with a ss in first picot at right end of edging, *make 3ch, then with RS of flower facing work 1ss in ch sp at tip of one petal of flower, 1ch, 1sc in each of the 3 chs of the 3-ch group, join with a ss in same picot.

Fasten off A.

Skip the next picot (at the center of the flower position—the one above the 3dcCL) and join A with a ss in next picot, *make 3ch, skip next petal on flower and work 1ss in ch sp at tip of next petal, 1ch, 1sc in each of the 3 chs of the 3-ch group, join with a ss in same picot.

Fasten off A.

Continue to join each flower over 3 picots in this way along edging, skipping 3 picots between the flowers, and adding the last flower over the last 3 picots.

Edging chart

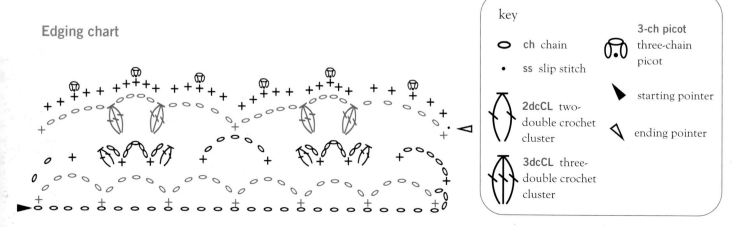

key

○ **ch** chain

• **ss** slip stitch

2dcCL two-double crochet cluster

3dcCL three-double crochet cluster

3-ch picot three-chain picot

▶ starting pointer

◁ ending pointer

Workshop 14

Using mohair and making tassels

Mohair yarn is a hairy yarn, which makes it difficult to crochet with because it is more difficult to see the individual stitches. The techniques in this Workshop will help to make sure that your mohair projects are successful—and once you are confident you can try the beautiful Scarf. This Workshop also covers some tips for choosing colors and how to make tassels.

Mohair

Mohair comes from the angora goat—not to be confused with the angora rabbit, which provides angora yarn. Mohair is often mixed with silk to create a soft yarn. It dyes well and comes in some beautiful colors.

Since it is hairy, it is hard to see the stitches in mohair yarn and the fibers also get very tangled, which makes it hard to undo if you make a mistake. To avoid problems it's essential to practice the stitches or motifs you're going to use beforehand using standard light worsted (double knitting/DK) or worsted (Aran) weight yarn. The hairy nature of the yarn also means that intricate and fine stitch patterns get lost, but using a larger hook will give projects enough volume and warmth. When crocheting in mohair, it is important to work very loosely to ensure that all the long fibers are drawn through the loops.

Tassels and fringes

Tassels are single clusters of knotted yarn ends; if they are repeated close together along an edge this creates a fringe. Use the same color yarn as for your project, or choose a contrast color of your choice.

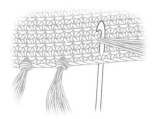

1 Cut strands of yarn to the length given in the pattern. Take one or more strands and fold in half. With the right side of the project facing, insert a crochet hook in one of the edge stitches from the wrong side. Catch the bunch of strands with the hook at the fold point.

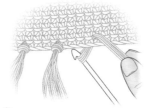

2 Draw all the loops through the stitch.

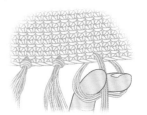

3 Pull through to make a big loop and, using your fingers, pull the tails of the bunch of strands through the loop.

4 Pull on the tails to tighten the loop firmly to secure the tassel.

TIP
When adding tassels to a foundation row, make sure that you pick up at least two loops of the crochet piece and not just one loop of the foundation chain, otherwise the loop will become loose and not hold the tassel securely.

Motif for scarf

Here is the motif used in the shawl project in this Workshop, so you can practice it using standard light worsted (DK) or worsted (Aran) weight yarn before attempting it in mohair.

Foundation ring: Using first color, make 4ch and join with a ss in first ch to form a ring.

Round 1 (RS): 1ch, 8sc in ring, join with a ss in first sc. *8 sc.*
Cont in rounds with RS always facing toward you.

Round 2: 3ch, 2dcCL in same place as last ss (counts as 3dcCL), [3ch, 3dcCL in next sc] 7 times, 3ch, join with a ss in top of first 3-ch. *8 clusters.* Cut off first color.

Round 3: Join second color in loop on hook, 3ch, 1dc in same place as ss (counts as 2dcCL), *skip 3 ch, [2dcCL, 5ch, 2dcCL] in top of next 3dcCL; rep from * 6 times more, 2dcCL in same place as first dc of round, 5ch, join with a ss in top of first 3-ch. *Eight 5-ch sps.* Cut off second color.

Round 4: Join third color in loop on hook, 7ch (counts as 1dc and 4ch), [1sc in next 5-ch sp, 4ch, skip next 2dcCL, 1dc in next 2dcCL, 4ch] 7 times, 1sc in next 5-ch sp, 4ch, join with a ss in 3rd of first 7-ch. *Sixteen 4-ch sps.*

Round 5: Continue with third color, 1ch, 1sc in same place as last ss, *4ch, skip 4 ch, [1tr, 3ch, 1tr] in next sc, 4ch, skip 4 ch, 1sc in next dc, 4ch, skip 4 ch, 1hdc in next sc, 4ch, skip 4 ch, 1sc in next dc; rep from * 3 times more omitting sc at end of last rep, join with a ss in first sc.

Round 6: Continue with third color, 1ch, 1sc in same place as last ss, 4sc in next ch sp, *[1dc, 3ch, 1dc] in next ch sp (corner), 4sc in next ch sp, 1sc in next sc, 4sc in next ch sp, 1sc in next hdc, 4sc in next ch sp, 1sc in next sc, 4sc in next ch sp; rep from * twice more, [1dc, 3ch, 1dc] in next ch sp (corner), 4sc in next ch sp, 1sc in next sc, 4sc in next ch sp, 1sc in next hdc, 4sc in next ch sp, join with a ss in first sc.
Fasten off.

Motif chart

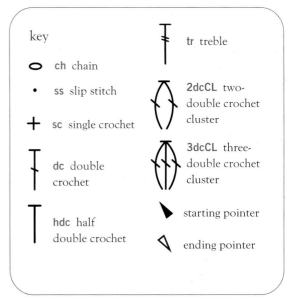

key

- **ch** chain
- **ss** slip stitch
- **sc** single crochet
- **dc** double crochet
- **hdc** half double crochet
- **tr** treble
- **2dcCL** two-double crochet cluster
- **3dcCL** three-double crochet cluster
- starting pointer
- ending pointer

Choosing color

The Scarf project that goes with this Workshop really showcases the colors you can get in a silk mohair. When choosing colors for a multi-color project like this I always start with one or two colors that I love. Choosing color is all about confidence—as far as I'm concerned there are no rules. There are color wheels and color theories, but my advice is to throw these away, because they can often knock your confidence. It doesn't matter if colors clash—think of all the beautiful oranges, pinks, and reds from India; in

theory these should look terrible, but they don't, they look vibrant and interesting. Crocheting with color is all part of the fun. My only advice is that when choosing a range of paler colors, try to bring in one of the colors from the yellow, green, or red palette that is a little brighter than the pales—you will find that this will lift the pale colors and show them off better. Colors are a very personal choice and so just have the confidence to go for it.

Mohair Scarf

This scarf is a real show stopper—the first time I wore it three people said it was the loveliest scarf they'd seen, so it's well worth the time and effort required. It's made using a mohair silk mix, which offers some beautiful colors to choose from.

techniques used

Stitches—single crochet, half double crochet, double crochet, trebles

Making lace-style squares

Making clusters

Joining squares with single crochet seams

scarf measurements

Finished scarf measures approximately 15¾ in. (40 cm) wide x 72 in. (183cm) long.

yarns

Debbie Bliss *Angel* (76% mohair, 24% silk) lace-weight yarn
1 x 25g (⅞oz) ball—approx. 200m (219yd)—of each of eleven colors:

36 Heather (light purple)
13 Coral
28 Basil (dark green)
17 Plum (dark purple)
03 Charcoal (dark gray)
12 Lime (pale green)
06 Ecru (off-white)
23 Kingfisher (teal blue)
19 Rose (pale pink)
14 Tangerine
09 Aqua (pale blue)

hook

3.5mm (US size E-4) crochet hook

gauge

Each square measures 5¼ x 5¼ in. (13 x 13 cm) using a US size E-4 (3.5 mm) crochet hook.

abbreviations

ch	chain
dc	double crochet
hdc	half double crochet
rep	repeat
sc	single crochet
sp(s)	space(s)
ss	slip stitch
st(s)	stitch(es)
tr	treble
RS	right side
yoh	yarn over hook

special abbreviations

2dcCL (two-double crochet cluster): [yoh, insert hook in st, yoh, pull yarn through work, yoh, pull yarn through first 2 loops on hook] twice in same st (3 loops now on hook), yoh and pull yarn through all 3 loops on hook to complete 2dcCL.

3dcCL (three-double crochet cluster): [yoh, insert hook in st, yoh, pull yarn through work, yoh, pull yarn through first 2 loops on hook] 3 times in same st (4 loops now on hook), yoh, pull yarn through all 4 loops on hook to complete the 3dcCL.

color combinations

The scarf is made up of a total of 42 squares. Each square uses three different colors, chosen at random.

Square motif chart

key

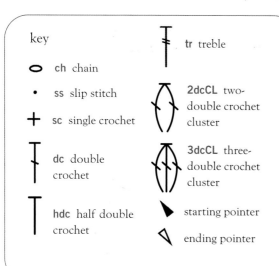

- **ch** chain
- **ss** slip stitch
- **sc** single crochet
- **dc** double crochet
- **hdc** half double crochet
- **tr** treble
- **2dcCL** two-double crochet cluster
- **3dcCL** three-double crochet cluster
- ► starting pointer
- ◁ ending pointer

TIPS

- Sew in yarn ends after making each square, using a yarn sewing needle.
- When adding tassels to a foundation row, make sure that you pick up at least two loops of the crochet piece and not just one loop of the foundation chain, otherwise the loop will become loose and not hold the tassel securely.

To make the squares

(Make 42)

Foundation ring: Using first color, make 4ch and join with a ss in first ch to form a ring.

Round 1 (RS): 1ch, 8sc in ring, join with a ss in first sc. *8 sc.* Cont in rounds with RS always facing you.

Round 2: 3ch, 2dcCL in same place as last ss (counts as 3dcCL), [3ch, 3dcCL in next sc] 7 times, 3ch, join with a ss in top of first 3-ch. *8 clusters.*
Cut off first color.

Round 3: Join second color in loop on hook, 3ch, 1dc in same place as ss (counts as 2dcCL), *skip 3 ch, [2dcCL, 5ch, 2dcCL] in top of next 3dcCL; rep from * 6 times more, 2dcCL in same place as first dc of round, 5ch, join with a ss in top of first 3-ch. *Eight 5-ch sps.*
Cut off second color.

Round 4: Join third color in loop on hook, 7ch (counts as 1dc and 4ch), [1sc in next 5-ch sp, 4ch, skip next 2dcCL, 1dc in next 2dcCL, 4ch] 7 times, 1sc in next 5-ch sp, 4ch, join with a ss in 3rd of first 7-ch. *Sixteen 4-ch sps.*

Round 5: Continue with third color, 1ch, 1sc in same place as last ss, *4ch, skip 4 ch, [1tr, 3ch, 1tr] in next sc, 4ch, skip 4 ch, 1sc in next dc, 4ch, skip 4 ch, 1hdc in next sc, 4ch, skip 4 ch, 1sc in next dc; rep from * 3 times more omitting sc at end of last rep, join with a ss in first sc.

Round 6: Continue with third color, 1ch, 1sc in same place as last ss, 4sc in next ch sp, *[1dc, 3ch, 1dc] in next ch sp (corner), 4sc in next ch sp, 1sc in next sc, 4sc in next ch sp, 1sc in next hdc, 4sc in next ch sp, 1sc in next sc, 4sc in next ch sp; rep from * twice more, [1dc, 3ch, 1dc] in next ch sp (corner), 4sc in next ch sp, 1sc in next sc, 4sc in next ch sp, 1sc in next hdc, 4sc in next ch sp, join with a ss in first sc.
Fasten off.

To finish the scarf

Arrange the squares in three rows of 14 squares each, in a random color order. With wrong sides together and using light purple (36 Heather), join the squares together using a single crochet seam. First join the 14 squares in each of the three rows, then join the rows.

To make the edging

With RS facing, join light purple (36 Heather) with a ss in center of 3-ch at one corner of scarf, 1ch, 2sc in same place, 1sc in each st and 1sc in each join along scarf edge to center ch at next corner, *2sc in center ch, 1sc in each st along scarf edge to center ch at next corner; rep from * to end, join with a ss in first sc.
Fasten off.

To make the tassels

Cut 50 strands 17 in. (43 cm) long of each of these five colors—off-white (06 Ecru), pale green (12 Lime), light purple (36 Heather), pale pink (19 Rose), and pale blue (09 Aqua).
Attach 25 tassels along each edge (see page 112). Attach the first tassel in a corner sc of edging and then a tassel in every subsequent third sc to next corner, attach last tassel in corner sc.

Workshop 15

Making toys

Making a toy usually involves working with simple stitches such as a single crochet or half double crochet, but the skill is in putting the toy together to create something cute and cuddly. Toys are usually made up of components and in the pattern that goes with this Workshop I have designed some cute Amigurumi bears. Amigurumi is the term used for the Japanese trend of making and stuffing small knitted or crocheted animals, but the techniques are the same if you are making a larger toy.

Amigurumi

Amigurumis are made in the round using the spiral technique (see Workshop 6, page 62) and it's important to remember to always use a stitch marker. Your gauge is not important when making toys and it's difficult to gauge anyway because when you stuff the toy the yarn and your stitches will stretch to different degrees, depending on whether you stuff loosely or tightly.

I like to use a soft yarn for toys. Generally we make them to give people as gifts or for a child, and who wants to cuddle up to an itchy or scratchy toy? The quantity of yarn for the Amigurumi is so small it's worth investing in a yarn that is soft.

Making the shape

To create the toy shape you need to increase and decrease by either single crocheting two stitches in one stitch (increase, see Workshop 3, Working in the Round, page 42) or single crocheting two stitches together into one stitch (decrease, see Getting Started, page 21).

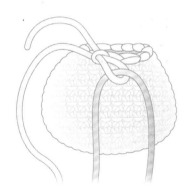

Round 1 (RS): Make 2ch, then work 6sc in 2nd ch from hook.

Round 2: Skip first sc, 2sc in each sc to end.
12 sc
The loop on the hook counts as one stitch in this technique, so the last stitch in the round is the one where the stitch marker is. Remember to keep moving the marker to mark the beginning of each round.

Continue to follow the pattern increasing on each row in the sequence indicated and then decreasing to create a tube. It's important to count the stitches at the end of each row, otherwise it could put your sequences out of line.

Eyes

I always think that—even though you may not be giving it to a child—the toy may end up in a child's hands, so I always use safety eyes. If you prefer you can embroider eyes after the toy is completed, but don't use beads that may come off. While the opening is still big enough, insert the safety eyes in place on the face and secure. The eyes sit between Rounds 4 and 5 of this pattern and about 9–11 stitches apart.

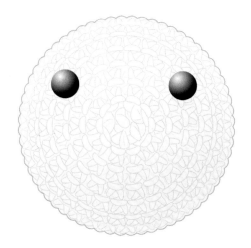

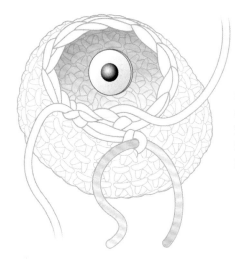

Insert the eye from the front and make sure they are completely level and sitting on the same row before you secure the safety catches at the back. The flat piece of the safety catch is pushed toward the crochet piece from the inside.

Stuffing

Use washable polyester filling that has a fire safety standard number and is available in most craft stores—usually in white. If you are making a dark colored toy, you may be able to find a darker color filling that will not show through as much.

Before you stuff the head, sew in the end from the beginning of the round on the inside of the toy because you won't be able to do this once the toy is stuffed.

Before working the last round, stuff the head lightly. I prefer not to put too much stuffing in my toys—I like them to be squidgy and soft. If you over stuff them, the toys will be hard and the stitches will stretch so much that you will be able to see the stuffing from the outside.

When you have stuffed the toy close the hole by decreasing in the last round. You can either decrease by making sc2tog around or skip 1 st, 1sc in the next st as below:
Round 13: *Skip 1 sc, 1sc in next sc; rep from * to end. *6 sc.*
Fasten off leaving a long tail. Weave around the last round with a yarn darning needle to close any hole that is left.
Make the body using the same techniques and following the pattern. Make the Ears in the same way as the head and body and sew in the end neatly from Round 1 to neaten any gaps.

Arms and legs

Arms and legs are small and fiddly, but remember to keep moving the stitch marker and counting the stitches in the round to ensure you have an even "tube." When you have fastened off, the end of the arm or leg can look a little messy. Thread the yarn end into a yarn sewing needle and weave it in and out to neaten up the ends of legs and arms—just doing this simple weaving can create the effect of a foot or hand.

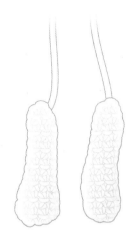

To finish the bear

Using a yarn sewing needle, weave in the yarn ends on the head, using the ends to neatly close the starting and finishing holes if necessary. Leave the long yarn ends (left when fastening off) on the body, arms, legs and ears to sew the pieces to each other. Weave in the other yarn ends on the body, arms, legs.

Pinning pieces together

Use long plastic-headed pins to pin the pieces together.

Head and body

Pin the head to the body, making sure that you center the head over the top of the body so the head is straight and not crooked.

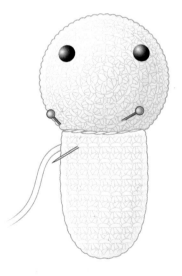

Sew the body to the head with a whipping stitch, using the long tail left when fastening off. Pick up the stitches in the last row of the body and the corresponding stitches above in the head. If the head looks crooked, use the needle and yarn end to make some more stitches until the head is sitting straight and secure.

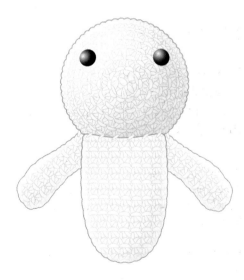

Pin the arms at the side of the body, at the join between the body and the head. Sew in place at the top of the body using long ends, stitching around the shoulders and top of the arms only.

Legs

Hold the toy upside down. Place the legs on the second round, on the sides, and pin and sew in place.

Ears

Place the ears with the yarn tail toward the head, then pin and sew in place about 3 rows back from the eye, on the side of the head and with about 8 rows between the ears.

Face details

Cut a circle of felt for the muzzle felt about 1 in. (2.5 cm) in diameter and a small oval for the nose about ¾ in. (1 cm). Pin the nose to the upper part of the muzzle and sew with a whipping stitch, using cotton thread and a sewing needle.

TIP

If you don't have embroidery floss pull apart a strand of yarn and use a thread from that. I tend to do this because I've always got scraps of yarn around rather than embroidery floss. To pull a thread off a piece of yarn, cut a piece of yarn 6–9 in. (15–22.5 cm), pull the ends apart, hold one strand with one hand, the other strands in the other hand and pull the strand apart.

The mouth is made using either two or three strands of embroidery floss. If you have a sewing needle with a large enough eye for the floss, use this, if not a yarn sewing needle with a sharp end will do. Sew one large stitch horizontally across the muzzle and fasten off.

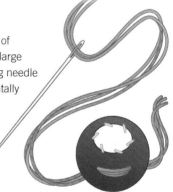

Pin the muzzle in the center of the face and, using a sewing thread to match the color of the muzzle, make whipping stitches around the edge to sew the muzzle onto the face.

Additional decorations

Decorate your toy however you like! Thread beads onto a piece of cotton thread and secure around the neck; use a ribbon around the head and tie in a bow or whatever decoration suits your toy. I once made a "Nicki" toy—I dressed it in a miniature version of a typical dress that I would wear in a color that I liked. I was wearing a lot of headscarves at the time, so I tied a ribbon round the head to look like a scarf.

Will and Rebecca bear

These cute little bears are a lot of fun to make. Every toy I make is always unique and develops its own character. If using a dark color yarn for the bear keep an eye on the stitches because they can be difficult to see—and make sure you have a good light when working.

techniques used

Stitches—single crochet

Amigurumi techniques

Increasing and decreasing with single crochet

Stuffing toys

Attaching toy safety eyes

Sewing on felt details with overcast stitches

Working backstitch facial features

Sewing together to create a professional-looking toy

bear measurements

Finished bears are approximately 6 in. (15 cm) tall.

yarns

Debbie Bliss *Rialto DK* (100% extra-fine merino wool superwash) light worsted (DK) weight yarn

Rebecca Bear:
1 x 1¾oz (50g) ball—approx. 115yd (105m)—of 42 Pink (light pink) or 66 Vintage Pink (pale pink)
Will Bear:
1 x 1¾oz (50g) ball—approx. 115yd (105m)—of 05 Chocolate (dark brown)

hook

US size G-6 (4 mm) crochet hook

extras

Both bears:
Safety-standard toy stuffing
Pair of black safety eyes, ⅜ in. (9 mm) in diameter

Rebecca Bear:
White felt, for muzzle
Bright pink felt, for nose
10 in. (25 cm) of flower print ribbon, ⅜ in. (1 cm) wide, for headband
Sewing threads to match felts and ribbon
Red cotton embroidery floss, for mouth
Round red seed beads, ¼ in. (6 mm) in diameter, for necklace

Will Bear:
Beige felt, for muzzle
Light pink felt, for nose
Sewing threads to match felts
Black cotton embroidery thread, for mouth

gauge

It is not necessary to work to an exact gauge when making crochet toys.

abbreviations

ch	chain
cont	continu(e)(ing)
rep	repeat
RS	right side
sc	single crochet
tog	together

special abbreviation

sc2tog (single crochet 2 together decrease): [Insert hook in next st, yoh and pull yarn through work] twice (3 loops now on hook), yoh and pull through all 3 loops on hook to complete the sc2tog decrease.

safety note for toys

These toys, and especially the added beads and ribbon, are not suitable for babies and very young children.

To make the bear's head

Using the pink yarn for Rebecca Bear or the brown yarn for Will Bear, make a ball-like shape in a spiral for the head as follows:
Round 1 (RS): Make 2ch, then work 6sc in 2nd ch from hook. Mark the beginning of each round and cont in rounds with RS always facing you.
Round 2: 2sc in each sc to end. *12 sc.*
Remember to keep moving the marker to mark the beginning of each round.
Round 3: *1sc in next sc, 2sc in next sc; rep from * to end. *18 sc.*
Round 4: *1sc in each of next 2 sc, 2sc in next sc; rep from * to end. *24 sc.*
Round 5: *1sc in each of next 3 sc, 2sc in next sc; rep from * to end. *30 sc.*
Round 6: *1sc in each of next 4 sc, 2sc in next sc; rep from * to end. *36 sc.*
Round 7: 1sc in each sc to end.
Round 8: *1sc in each of next 4 sc, sc2tog; rep from * to end. *30 sc.*
Round 9: *1sc in each of next 3 sc, sc2tog; rep from * to end. *24 sc.*
Round 10: *1sc in each of next 2 sc, sc2tog; rep from * to end. *18 sc.*
Round 11: 1sc in each sc to end.
Round 12: *1sc in next sc, sc2tog; rep from * to end. *12 sc.*
While the opening is still large enough, insert the safety eyes in place on the face and secure. The eyes sit between Rounds 4 and 5 of this pattern and approximately 9–11 sts apart.
Before working the last round, stuff the head lightly.
Round 13: *Skip 1 sc, 1sc in next sc; rep from * to end. *6 sc.*
Fasten off.

To make the bear's body

Using the pink yarn for Rebecca Bear or the brown yarn for Will Bear, make an oblong shape in a spiral for body as follows:
Rounds 1, 2 and 3: Work as for Rounds 1, 2 and 3 of Head. Remember to keep moving the marker to mark the beginning of each round.
Rounds 4–10: 1sc in each sc to end. *18 sc.*
Before working the last round, stuff the body.
Round 11: Dc2tog to end. *9 sc.*
Fasten off, leaving a long yarn end.

To make the bear's arms

(Make two)
Using the pink yarn for Rebecca Bear or the brown yarn for Will Bear, make a tube-like shape in a spiral for arm as follows:
Round 1 (RS): Make 2ch, then work 6sc in 2nd ch from hook. Mark the beginning of each round and cont in rounds with RS always facing you.
Round 2: 1sc in each sc to end. *6 sc.*
Remember to keep moving the marker to mark the beginning of each round.
Repeat Round 2 until arm measures 1½ in. (4 cm).
Fasten off, leaving a long yarn end.
Do not stuff.

To make the bear's legs

(Make two)
Using the pink yarn for Rebecca Bear or the brown yarn for Will Bear, make a tube-like shape in a spiral for leg as follows:
Round 1 (RS): Make 2ch, then work 6sc in 2nd ch from hook. Mark the beginning of each round and cont in rounds with RS always facing you.
Round 2: 1sc in each sc to end. *6 sc.*
Remember to keep moving the marker to mark the beginning of each round.
Repeat Round 2 until leg measures 1¼ in. (3 cm).
Fasten off, leaving a long yarn end.
Do not stuff.

To make the bear's ears

(Make two)
Using the pink yarn for Rebecca Bear or the brown yarn for Will Bear, make a circle in a spiral for ear as follows:
Round 1 (RS): Make 2ch, then work 6sc in 2nd ch from hook. Mark the beginning of each round and cont in rounds with RS always facing you.
Round 2: 2sc in each sc to end. *12 sc.*
Remember to keep moving the marker to mark the beginning of each round.
Round 3: 1sc in each sc to end.
Fasten off, leaving a long yarn end.
Sew in the yarn end from Round 1 to neaten any gaps.

To finish the bear

Sew in the yarn ends, sew the bear pieces together, and add the face details as explained on page 120.

Accessories for Rebecca Bear

Thread the beads onto a long doubled length of sewing thread, tie the beads around the neck and knot, then sew them in place at the back of the neck.
Place the ribbon around the head in front of the ears, and tie in a bow at the front. Trim the ends, then pin and sew in place with sewing thread.

Workshop 16

Intarsia

To create a picture or colored motif in crochet you must use the intarsia method. The motif can be seen on both sides of the work, but there is still a right and wrong side. The colors are carried up the rows of the motif without being cut and without carrying them across the work, which means the work will just have one thickness of yarn and no bulky strands across the back. For this Workshop, I have designed an Intarsia Heart Pillow cover.

Working intarsia

Intarsia is often worked in single crochet, which is the most dense and untextured stitch. The turning chain at the end of each row is one chain for single crochet—if you're working in another stitch use the correct number of turning chains.

The pretty pillow cover which forms the project at the end of this workshop is made up of nine

small squares, each with a heart motif in the center. Two balls of color A are used for the background of each square and one ball of color B for the motif. Colors are joined in the normal way in the last part of the previous stitch (see Getting Starting, Joining in a New Ball of Yarn, page 23).

Intarsia charts

A chart for intarsia looks like a graph—each square of the chart represents one single stitch horizontally and one row vertically. The chart is read first from right to left on the first row and then from left to right on the second and so on. It's important to mark off the chart as you go; I tend to mark off the rows with a colored pen or pencil to make the chart more readable. It's always best to photocopy a copy of the chart from the book, so you can scribble all over it.

Heart motif chart

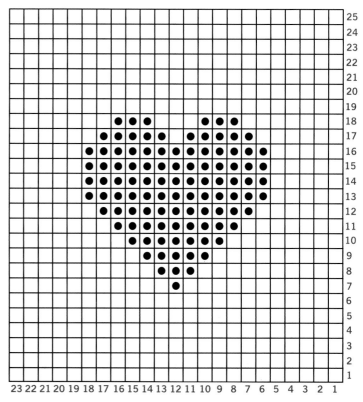

Intarsia heart pattern

Before you start on the pattern, print off the chart and wind off two balls of color A from one larger ball. Cut a separate strand of yarn about 40 in. (100 cm) long to be used for the indentation at the top of the heart.

TIP
Keep the first stitch of the motif loose. Color B of the motif in the first row can get a bit lost or look off center if stitches are pulled too tightly. Count stitches on either side of the motif to check you have the stitches of the motif in the center.

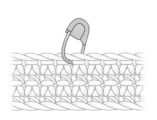

1 Using color A (ball 1), make the Foundation chain and follow the chart by single crocheting the one-color rows leading up to the motif, making sure you make the 1 turning chain at the end of each row. When you are ready to start the motif, place a stitch marker in the center stitch of the row.

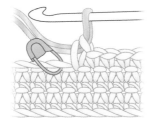

2 Work the beginning of the row in color A to the stitch before the stitch marker.
Motif row 1 (RS): Join in color B in the stitch before the stitch marker.

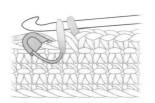

3 Drop color A (ball 1), insert the hook in the next stitch (with stitch marker), pull the yarn through the stitch with color B.

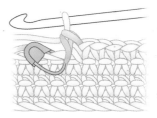

4 Take color A (ball 2), drop color B, pull the yarn through both loops to complete the single crochet stitch.

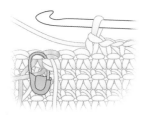

5 Continue in single crochet with color A (ball 2), to the end of the row, leaving color A (ball 1) and color B behind and sitting at the back of the work (wrong side).
Motif row 2 (WS): Make the turning chain and turn for the next row. Using color A (ball 2), single crochet up to two stitches before color B (with the stitch marker).

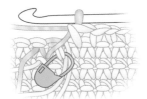

6 Insert the hook into the next stitch of color A (ball 2), pull the yarn through the stitch. Drop color A (ball 2) and bring the strand of color A (ball 2) over the top of the work to drape on the wrong side (facing you). Bring up the strand of color B loosely across and join by pulling it through both loops on the hook.

7 Insert the hook into the next stitch, gently pushing the strand of color B out of the way.

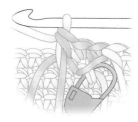

8 Complete the stitch using color B. Make one single crochet in the next stitch using color B. Insert the hook in the next stitch (of motif pattern using color B), pull the yarn through the stitch. Drop color B, keeping the strand of yarn on the wrong side (facing you), pick up color A (ball 1) and complete the stitch. All strands should be on the wrong side (facing you).

Continue using only one of the balls from color A to the end of the row, keeping ball 1 always on one side of the motif and ball 2 on the other side.

Crochet the motif using this technique and following the color guidance on the chart, changing the color in the top of the stitch before the motif color (color B) is needed. Always make sure that you keep all the strands on the wrong side of the work and work strands at the side of the motif loosely.

At Row 11 of the heart motif, bring in the strand of color A that you cut and put aside earlier to work the last two rows of the indentation at the center of the heart. Use the same intarsia technique. Continue to complete the chart using the same technique as before and complete the intarsia motif square.

Intarsia Heart Pillow

Intarsia is not as frightening as it may seem! These hearts demonstrate the intarsia method perfectly and are not too big a project to master. They look so pretty in a pillow, which would make a lovely gift for someone who has just moved into a new home. Try out different color schemes—if you make the hearts in red it also makes a great Valentine's Day present.

techniques used

Stitches—single crochet

Making an intarsia motif

Changing colors in intarsia

Working from an intarsia chart

Joining squares with a single crochet seam

pillow cover measurements

Finished pillow cover fits a pillow form 16 in. (40 cm) square.

yarns

Debbie Bliss *Rialto DK* (100% extra-fine merino wool superwash) light worsted (DK) weight yarn

4 x 1¾oz (50g) ball—approx. 460yd (420m)—of main color:

MC 04 Gray

1 x 1¾oz (50g) ball—approx. 115yd (105m)—of each of three contrasting colors:

A 58 Grass (green)

B 50 Deep Rose (pink)

C 45 Gold (yellow)

hook

US size E-4 (3.5mm) crochet hook

extras

16 in. (40 cm) square pillow form

gauge

17 sts x 18 rows over a 4 in. (10 cm) square worked in single crochet using a US size E-4 (3.5 mm) hook.

abbreviations

ch	chain
cont	continu(e)(ing)
MC	main color
rep	repeat
RS	right side
sc	single crochet
st(s)	stitch(es)

color combinations

The cushion front is made up of a total of 9 squares.

Always use MC as the background color. Make three squares with the heart motif in A, three with the heart motif in B and three with the heart motif in C.

To make the heart squares

(Make a total of 9 squares)

Foundation chain: Using MC, make 24ch.

Row 1 (RS): 1sc in 2nd ch from hook, 1sc in each ch to end. *23 sc.*

Row 2: 1ch (does not count as a st), 1sc in each sc to end. *23 sc.*

Rows 3–6: Rep Row 2.

Cont in sc throughout, following chart for Rows 7–18 to work the heart motif and using one small ball of MC on each side of the motif.

Using MC only, work 7 rows more in sc.

Fasten off.

To make the striped pillow-cover back

Foundation chain: Using MC, make 70ch.

Row 1: 1sc in 2nd ch from hook, 1sc in each st to end. *69 sc.*

Row 2: 1ch (does not count as a st), 1sc in each sc to end. *69 sc.*

Rep Row 2 for 4 rows more.

Cut off MC, but do not fasten off.

Cont in sc, working 67 rows more in a random stripe sequence with colors MC, A, B and C for a total of 73 rows. Alternatively, work the remaining 67 rows of stripes in the following sequence: 6 rows A, 6 rows B, 5 rows C, 4 rows MC, 6 rows A, 5 rows C, 5 rows MC, 6 rows B, 5 rows C, 4 rows MC, 5 rows A, 6 rows B, 4 rows MC. Fasten off.

To join the heart squares together

Using a yarn sewing needle, sew in all yarn ends on the back panel and the heart squares. Then join the heart squares together using MC (gray) and a single crochet seam (see Workshop 3, Single crochet seam, page 43) with wrong sides of squares together, so the seams will show on the right side of the pillow. First join together the three squares with A (green) hearts, the three squares with B (pink) hearts, and the three squares with C (yellow) hearts, to form the three horizontal rows. Then join together the three horizontal rows to make a nine-square pillow-front panel—with the A hearts at the top, the B hearts in the middle, and the C hearts at the bottom.

To finish the pillow cover

Make a single crochet seam around the pillow-cover front and back as follows:

With wrong sides together, pin the pillow front and back panels together, leaving the top edge open. Join MC with a ss in top left-hand corner, inserting hook through front and back pieces, 1ch, 3sc in corner st, 23sc evenly along side of each of the three squares (skipping the seam joins), 3sc in corner st, 23sc along bottom of each of the three squares (skipping the seam joins), 3sc in corner st, 23sc evenly along side of each square (skipping the seam joins). Do not fasten off.

Insert the pillow form, then make 23sc along top of each of the three squares (skipping the seam joins), join with a ss in top of first sc of round.

Fasten off.

Heart motif chart

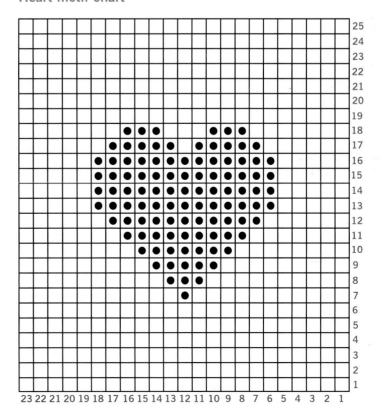

Workshop 17

Advanced pattern reading and shapings

Once you understand how to read a pattern, get the idea of the way abbreviations are written and know about asterisks and brackets, then understanding any pattern is just a case of practice and experience. With more complicated patterns you need to know exactly where you are in the pattern and to follow instructions meticulously, because even a small mistake can cause bigger problems down the line. This Workshop also includes a different way of working crochet rib, which is used for the cuffs on the project—a pair of Gloves—and how to make a simple crochet bow.

Advanced pattern reading

In all the workshops so far we have shown you how to read the pattern so this Workshop just takes things a step further. The Gloves pattern that goes with this Workshop is not made in a difficult or complicated stitch—it's just single crochet. But it's important that you read the pattern line by line and mark off each row.

The gloves are worked in a spiral and it is vital that you turn the work at the end of each row and then commence the next row going back over the stitches you've just made in the other direction. This avoids a line showing up the glove where each round starts and finishes. A stitch marker is essential and you must also be confident in counting stitches. This patterns calls for precision and it's important to pick up and work on the exact amount of stitches in the pattern.

The glove fits an average sized woman's hand and is made using a fine yarn. If you would like a larger glove, either make the fingers longer by crocheting more rounds before the decrease for the finger tips, or try using a larger hook and a thicker yarn for a glove that is larger all round.

Use whatever technique suits you best to mark where you are in the pattern—photocopy and print off your pattern so you can scribble over it. To keep tabs on when you are, try using a big colored plastic-headed pin in the side of your page to mark the row you are working on, or mark off your rows with a pen or pencil.

Cuffs and ribs

Crochet ribs are not as common as they are in knitting, but they are useful when you would like your stitches to be dense but still have some stretch in them. You can use a raised stitch as a rib (see Workshop 6, Creating crochet rib, page 63) or the technique I have used for the cuff in the Gloves project. This involves crocheting in the back loops of single crochet and then, when the work has the right length, turning it round and creating stitches along the long edge so that the main part of the glove can then be worked up into the fingers.

Making a ribbed cuff

Make 11ch, or the number of stitches you need for the width of the rib—on the Gloves, we are working on 10ch. The length required is the measurement that wraps around the wrist.

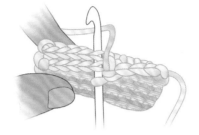

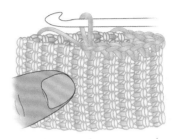

1 Make the cuff in single crochet stitches, making 1 turning ch and placing the hook into the back stitches only (not both loops). This creates small ridges.

2 The cuff is then joined at the short ends with a single crochet seam (see Workshop 3, Single crochet seam, page 43).

3 The cuff from here on is worked by single crocheting around the top edge and carrying on up to make the hand and the fingers.

Crochet bow

This pretty bow can be used to decorate many of your crochet projects.

Foundation chain: Using a US size D-3 (3 mm) hook and A, make 16ch and join with a ss in first ch to form a ring.
Round 1 (RS): 1ch (does not count as a st), 1sc in each sc to end, join with a ss in first sc. *16 sts.*
Do not turn at end of rounds, but cont with RS always facing.
Round 2: 3ch (counts as first dc), 1dc in each st to end; join with a ss in top of first 3-ch. *16 sts.*
Round 3: 1ch, 1sc in each st to end, join with a ss in first sc. Fasten off, leaving a yarn tail approx. 17½ in. (45 cm) long.

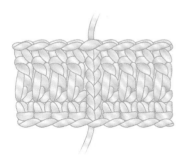

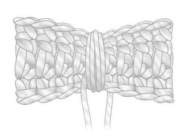

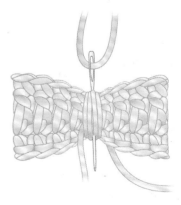

1 Turn the piece right side out and hold it flat with the fasten-off stitch and the tail at the top at center front.

2 Wrap the yarn tail tightly around the center of the ring to create a bow shape.

3 Thread the yarn tail into a yarn sewing needle and make a stitch on the reverse to secure it in place.

Cozy gloves

Crocheting in the round is the perfect way to make fingers for gloves. Once you've made one pair of these you'll be asked to make loads—they don't use up much yarn and they make great gifts. I've used a yarn that contains a mix of cashmere and merino wool and comes in lots of gorgeous colors. Crochet gloves can be bulky if you use a thick yarn, so if you'd like to make these bigger go for one yarn thickness up such as a double knit (DK) or an Aran.

To make the right glove

The Cuff is made in rows, then the short ends are joined (to fit around the wrist) and the Hand section is worked onto it in rounds.

Cuff (ribbing)

All stitches in the Cuff are to be made in the back loops only to form ribbing.

Foundation chain: Using a US size G-6 (4 mm) hook and MC, make 11ch.

Row 1 (RS): 1sc in 2nd ch from hook, 1sc in each of next 9 ch. *10 sts.*

Row 2: 1ch (does not count as a st), working into back loops only at top of each sc, work 1sc in each sc to end. *10 sts.*

Rows 3–25: Rep Row 2.

Do not fasten off.

Join cuff

Row 26: Fold Cuff in half widthways with RS together so that the short ends are aligned and the foundation chain edge is behind Row 25, then join the two layers with slip stitches, by working 1ss through top of each stitch in row below and through corresponding foundation chain behind it to end.

Turn Cuff right side out so slip stitch seam is on inside.

Hand

Note: It's important to turn at the end of each round to keep the join straight.

All stitches for the remainder of the glove are to be made in both loops. Place a stitch marker in the 1-ch at the beginning of each round.

Round 1 (RS): Using a US size G-6 (4 mm) hook and MC, 1ch (does not count as st), 1sc in end of each row of ribbing (26 sts), join with a ss in first 1-ch, turn.

techniques used

Stitches—single crochet, double crochet

Making crochet ribbing

Crocheting into back loop of top of stitch

Turning work at end of rounds

Making a slip stitch seam

Using advanced shaping techniques

glove measurements

To fit an average size woman's hand. Finished gloves measure approximately 9 in. (23 cm) long and approximately 3½ in. (9 cm) wide across one side of the hand section.

yarns

Debbie Bliss *Baby Cashmerino* (55% merino wool, 33% microfiber, 12% cashmere) lightweight (fine-weight) yarn

Gloves:
2 x 1¾oz (50g) balls—approx. 274yd (250m)—of main color:
MC 002 Apple (light green)
Bow:
1 x 1¾oz (50g) balls—approx. 137yd (125m)—of one color:
A 068 Peach Melba (peach)

hooks

US size D-3 (3 mm) crochet hook

US size G-6 (4 mm) crochet hook

gauge

18 sts x 20 rows over a 4 in. (10 cm) square worked in single crochet using a US size G-6 (4 mm) hook

abbreviations

ch	chain
cont	continu(e)(ing)
MC	main color
rep	repeat
RS	right side
sc	single crochet
ss	slip stitch
st(s)	stitch(es)
tog	together
WS	wrong side
yoh	yarn over hook

special abbreviation

sc2tog (single crochet 2 together decrease): [Insert hook in next st, yoh and pull yarn through work] twice (3 loops now on hook), yoh and pull through all 3 loops on hook to complete the sc2tog decrease.

Round 2 (WS): 1ch, 1sc in each of next 4 sts, 2sc in next st, 1sc in each of next 8 sts, 2sc in next st, 1sc in each of next 8 sts, 2sc in next st, 1sc in each of next 3 sts, join with a ss in first 1-ch (the 1-ch with stitch marker), turn. *29 sts.*

Round 3: 1ch (insert stitch marker), 1sc in each of next 29 sts, join with a ss in first 1-ch, turn. *29 sts.*

Rounds 4–14: Rep Round 3, ensuring that you turn at the end of each Round.

Round 15 (RS): 1ch, 1sc in each of next 15 sts, 5ch, skip next 5 sts (thumb opening), 1sc in each of next 9 sts, join with a ss in first 1-ch, turn.

Round 16: 1ch, 1sc in each of next 9 sts, 1sc in each of next 5 ch, 1sc in each of next 15 sts, join with a ss in first 1-ch, turn. *29 sts.*

Rounds 17–21: Rep Round 3. *29 sts.*

Do not turn at end of Round 21 (this is a RS round).

Start fingers

Place a stitch marker in first 1-ch at beginning of each round.

Little finger

Round 1 (RS): 1ch (does not count as st), 1sc in each of next 7 sts, 2ch, join with a ss in first sc of this round, turn. Working around the stitches in Round 1 only, cont as follows:

Round 2: 1ch, 1sc in each of 2 ch of previous round, 1sc in each of next 7 sts, join with a ss in first 1-ch, turn. *9 sts.*

Round 3: 1ch, 1sc in each of next 9 sts, join with a ss in first 1-ch, turn. *9 sts.*

Rounds 4–12: Rep Round 3. *9 sts.*

Round 13: 1ch, 1sc in first st, [sc2tog] 4 times, join with a ss in first 1-ch. *5 sts.*

Fasten off, leaving a long yarn tail.

Ring finger

With thumbhole on the left-hand side and the little finger on the right and starting on the row of stitches at the back layer of the glove (so you are working a WS row on the inside of the finger), join yarn with a ss in the next st after the 7th sc of the Little Finger in Round 1.

Round 1 (WS): 1ch, 1sc in same st, 1sc in each of next 2 sts, 2ch, 1sc in the third st from base of Little Finger on the other side of the glove, 1sc in each of next 2 sts, make 2sc along the base of the Little Finger, join with a ss in the first sc of this round, turn.

Round 2 (RS): 1ch, 1sc in each of next 5 sts, 1sc in each of the next 2 ch, 1sc in each of next 3 sts, join with a ss in first 1-ch, turn. *10 sts.*

Round 3: 1ch, 1sc in each of next 10 sts, join with a ss in first 1-ch, turn. *10 sts.*

Rounds 4–13: Rep Round 3. *10 sts.*

Round 14: 1ch, [sc2tog] 5 times, join with a ss in first 1-ch. *5 sts.* Fasten off, leaving a long yarn tail.

Middle finger

With thumbhole on the left-hand side and the fingers on the right and starting on the row of stitches at the back layer of the glove, join yarn with a ss in the next st after the first 3 sc of Ring Finger Round 1.

Round 1 (WS): 1ch, 1sc in same st, 1sc in each of the next 3 sts, 2ch.

Now turn glove around so that the stitches just worked are at the front.

1sc in the fourth sc from base of Ring Finger on other side of glove, 1sc in each of next 3 sts, make 2sc along base of Ring Finger, join with a ss in first sc, turn.

Round 2 (RS): 1ch, 1sc in each of next 6 sts, 1sc in each of the 2 ch, 1sc in each of next 4 sts, join with a ss in first 1-ch, turn. *12 sts.*

Round 3: 1ch, 1sc in each of the next 12 sts, join with a ss in first 1-ch, turn. *12 sts.*

Rounds 4–14: Rep Round 3. *12 sts.*

Round 15: 1ch, *1sc in next st, sc2tog; rep from * 3 times more, join with a ss in first 1-ch, turn. *8 sts.*

Round 16: 1ch, [sc2tog] 4 times, join with a ss in first 1-ch. *4 sts.* Fasten off, leaving a long yarn tail.

Index finger

With thumbhole on the left-hand side and the fingers on the right and starting on the row at the back of the glove, join yarn in the next sc after the first 4 sc of the Middle Finger in Round 1.

Round 1 (WS): 1ch, 1sc in same st, 1sc in each of next 7 sts, make 2sc along base of Middle Finger, join with a ss in first 1-ch, turn. *10 sts.*

Round 2: 1ch, 1sc in each of next 10 sts, join with a ss in first 1-ch, turn. *10 sts.*

Rounds 3–12: Rep Round 2. *10 sts.*

Round 13: 1ch, [sc2tog] 5 times, join with a ss in first 1-ch. *5 sts.* Fasten off, leaving a long yarn tail.

Thumb

With RS of thumbhole facing, join yarn with a ss to bottom of first chain on top edge of thumbhole.

Round 1 (RS): 1ch, 1sc in same st, 1sc in each of next 4 sts along top edge of thumb opening, 7sc evenly along the bottom edge of thumb opening, join with a ss in first sc, turn. *12 sts.*

Round 2: 1ch, 1sc in each of next 12 sts, join with a ss in first 1-ch, turn. *12 sts.*

Rounds 3–10: Rep Round 2. *12 sts.*

Round 11: 1ch, *1sc in next st, sc2tog; rep from * 3 times more, join with a ss in first 1-ch, turn. *8 sts.*

Round 12: 1ch, [sc2tog] 4 times, join with a ss in first 1-ch. *4 sts.* Fasten off, leaving a long yarn tail.

To make the left glove

Make exactly as for the Right Glove, EXCEPT do not turn right side

out before Hand is begun, so that cuff seam remains on outside of glove. This glove is worked inside out and turned right side out once the yarn ends are sewn in.

To finish the gloves

Turn the Right Glove inside out, passing the yarn ends to the wrong side, so that both gloves are now wrong side out. Note that the vertical "join" in the rounds of the Hand section are on the "palm" side of each glove.

Using a yarn sewing needle, weave the yarn tail through the stitches on last the round of each finger on the wrong side and pull tight to secure the closing. Sew in all the yarn ends, then turn each glove right side out.

To make the bows

(Make two)

Foundation chain: Using a US size D-3 (3 mm) hook and A, make 16ch and join with a ss in first ch to form a ring.

Round 1 (RS): 1ch (does not count as a st), 1sc in each sc to end, join with a ss in first sc. *16 sts.*

Do not turn at end of rounds, but cont with RS always facing.

Round 2: 3ch (counts as first dc), 1dc in each st to end; join with a ss in top of first 3-ch. *16 sts.*

Round 3: 1ch, 1sc in each st to end, join with a ss in first sc. Fasten off, leaving a yarn tail approx. 17½ in. (45 cm) long.

Turn right side out. Hold the piece flat with the fasten-off stitch and the tail at the top at the front center.

Wrap the yarn tail tightly around the center of the ring to create a bow shape, and secure in place with a yarn sewing needle.

Attach each Bow to the center front of the Glove, positioned at the wrist above the cuff ribbing.

Workshop 18

Triangular motifs and longer stitches

Making triangle motifs is very similar to making squares; they start out as circles and then the triangular shape emerges in later rounds. However, laying the triangles out and joining them to make a blanket takes a little more thought and skill. The project for this Workshop, a Blanket, is made using a fine fingering (4-ply) yarn and I've chosen a silk mix yarn for a very luxurious project. It not only uses triangular motifs but also double trebles to make an open and light center, and raised single crochet stitches for texture. This Workshop also covers working a decrease by working three double trebles together (dtr3tog).

Double trebles (dtr)

Double trebles are "tall" stitches and are an extension on the basic treble stitch. They need a turning chain of 5 chains.

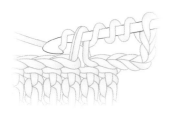

1 Yarn over hook three times, insert the hook into the stitch or space.

2 Yarn over hook, pull the yarn through the work (5 loops on hook).

3 Yarn over hook, pull the yarn through the first 2 loops on the hook (4 loops on hook).

4 Yarn over hook, pull the yarn through the first 2 loops on the hook (3 loops on hook).

5 Yarn over hook, pull the yarn through the first 2 loops on the hook (2 loops on hook).

6 Yarn over hook, pull the yarn through 2 loops on the hook (1 loop on hook). One double treble completed.

double treble (dtr) in symbols

Three-double treble cluster (3dtrCL)

This is a long stitch that requires a lot of wrapping round—make sure you have a long enough hook shaft. Some hooks have handles with small shafts which will make winding the yarn over the hook more difficult.

1 *Yarn over hook three times, insert the hook into the stitch or space, yarn over hook, pull the yarn through the work (5 loops on hook).

2 Yarn over hook, pull the yarn through the first two loops on the hook (4 loops on hook).

3 Yarn over hook, pull the yarn through the first two loops on the hook (3 loops on hook).

4 Yarn over hook, pull the yarn through the first two stitches on the hook (2 loops on hook).

three-double treble cluster (3dtrCL) in symbols

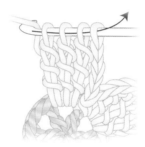 

5 Repeat from * once, leaving 3 loops on the hook.

6 Repeat from * once more, leaving 4 loops on the hook.

7 Yarn over hook, pull the yarn through all 4 loops on the hook (1 loop on hook). One three-double treble cluster completed.

Raised single crochet round front (sc/rf)

Raised single crochet stitches are made in the same way as raised doubles (see Workshop 6, Raised double round front, page 63) and are created by making stitches around the "posts" of the stitches below (in the previous round/row)—the posts are also sometimes called "stems" or "stalks". Here we are working around the front post.

raised single crochet round front (sc/rf) in symbols

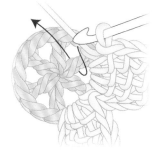 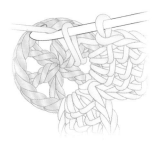 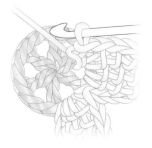

1 Insert the hook from the front and around the post (the stem) of next double from right to left.

2 yarn over hook, pull the yarn through the work, yarn round hook.

3 Pull the yarn through 2 loops on the hook (1 loop on hook). One front raised single crochet completed.

Triangular motifs

Each side of the triangle will measure the same and it's important to keep an eye on the stitch count along each side so that it does not go out of shape. I always block and steam triangle motifs, which makes them much easier to join.

Foundation ring: Using A, make 4ch and join in with a ss in first ch to form a ring.

Round 1 (RS): 5ch (counts as 1dc and 3ch), *[1dc in ring, 2ch] 5 times, join with a ss in 3rd of 5-ch at beg of round.

Fasten off A.

Cont in rounds with RS always facing you.

Round 2: Join B with a ss in top of any dc, *5ch, 3dtrCL in next 2-ch sp, 5ch, 1sc/rf around next dc from previous Round; rep from * 5 times more, join with a ss in same sp as joining st. Fasten off B.

Round 3: Join MC with a ss in top of any 3dtrCL from previous Round, 7ch (counts as 1tr and 3ch), 1tr in same st (corner), *3ch, 1dtr in next sc/rf, 3ch, 1sc in next 3dtrCL, 3ch, 1dtr in next sc/rf, 3ch, [1tr, 3ch, 1tr] (corner) in next 3dtrCL; rep from * once more, 3ch, 1dtr in next sc/rf, 3ch, 1sc in next 3dtrCL, 3ch, 1dtr in next sc/rf, 3ch, join with a ss in 4th of first 7-ch.

Round 4: Ss in next 3-ch sp, 6ch, (counts as 1dc and 3ch), 2dc in same ch sp (corner), *[1dc in next st, 3dc in next ch sp] 4 times**, 1dc in next st, [2dc, 3ch, 2dc] in corner sp*; rep from * to * once more, then work from * to **, 1dc in same place as ss at end of Round 3, 1dc in same sp as ss at beg of round, join with a ss in 3rd of first 6-ch. *21 dc on each side of triangle.*

Round 5: Ss in next 3-ch sp, 6ch (counts as 1dc and 3ch), 2dc in same ch sp (corner), *1dc in each dc to next corner sp, [2dc, 3ch, 2dc] in corner sp; rep from * once more, 1dc in each dc to next corner, 1dc in same place as ss at end of Round 4, 1dc in same corner sp as ss at beg of round, join with a ss in third of first 6-ch. *25 dc on each side of triangle.*
Fasten off.

Triangle motif chart

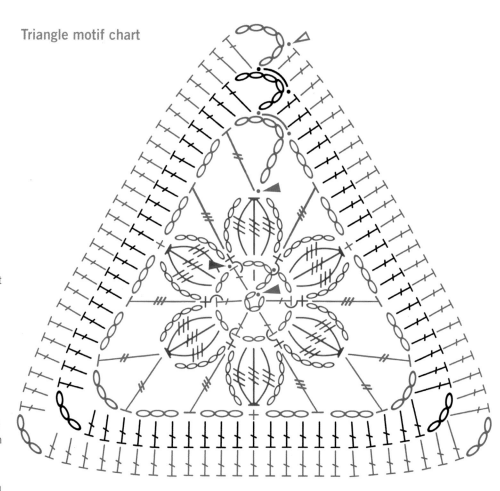

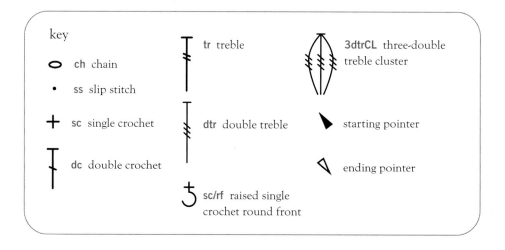

key

⬯ **ch** chain

• **ss** slip stitch

✚ **sc** single crochet

𝖳 **dc** double crochet

𝖳 **tr** treble

𝖳 **dtr** double treble

⌇ **sc/rf** raised single crochet round front

◗ **3dtrCL** three-double treble cluster

▶ starting pointer

▷ ending pointer

Joining triangles

When you have made all the triangles for the blanket, first sew in all the ends, then block and steam each triangle on the wrong side before laying out the blanket design. The easiest way to join lots of triangles is first to join them in strips and then to sew the strips together to make a larger piece.

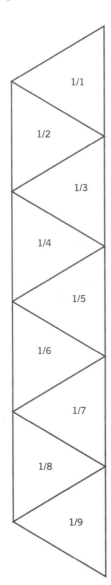

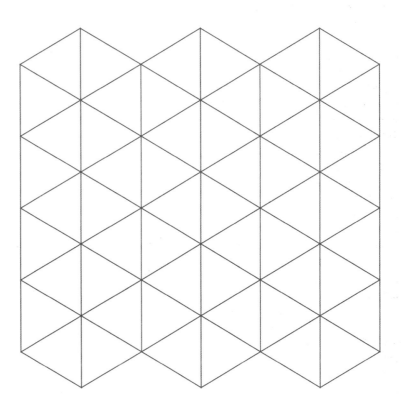

1 Lay out all the triangles on a flat surface, ensuring that you place the colors randomly, and then set them out in strips as in the diagram. Join the triangles together in strips using the overcast joining method (Workshop 2, Joining squares: Overcast method, page 37), with right sides together. Label each strip in rows 1 to 9 (or up to the number you have in a row).

2 When all the strips are joined, join the strips to each other to create the blanket—making sure that the points of each set of triangles meet in the center.

Triangle Blanket

This is a real special occasion blanket —a true piece of art—so take your time with it. Each motif has the same pattern, but uses a different color in the center, so if you are looking for a long-term project that you can just pick up and put down this blanket is ideal. I used my favorite silk blend yarn—if you choose something different, don't go thicker than a light worsted (DK).

techniques used

Stitches—single crochet, double crochet, trebles, and double trebles

Making triangles

blanket measurements

Finished blanket measures approximately 43¼ x 56¾ in. (110 x 144 cm).

yarns

Fyberspates *Scrumptious* 4-ply Sport (55% merino wool, 45% silk) super-fine-weight yarn
6 x 3½oz (100g) hanks—approx. 2,394yd (2,190m)—of main color:
MC 304 Water (gray-blue)

1 x 3½oz (100g) hanks—approx. 399yd (365m)—of each of four contrasting colors (for A, B):
314 Magenta (bright pink)
306 Baby Pink (pale pink)
302 Gold (gold)
311 Flying Saucer (pale green)

hook

US size E-4 (3.5 mm) crochet hook

gauge

Sides of triangle measure 6¼ in. (16 cm) using a US size E-4 (3.5 mm) hook.

abbreviations

beg	beginning
ch	chain
cont	continu(e)(ing)
dc	double crochet
dtr	double treble
MC	main color
rep	repeat
RS	right side
sc	single crochet
sp(s)	space(s)
ss	slip stitch
st(s)	stitch(es)
tr	treble
WS	wrong side
yoh	yarn over hook

special abbreviations

sc/rf (raised single crochet round front): Inserting hook from front, work 1sc around post of stitch.

3dtrCL (3-double treble cluster): *Yoh 3 times and insert hook in sp, yoh and pull yarn through work (5 loops on hook), [yoh and pull yarn through first two loops on hook] 3 times; rep from * twice more (4 loops now on hook), yoh and pull yarn through all 4 loops on hook to complete the 3dtrCL.

color combinations

The blanket is made up of a total of 136 triangles.

Always use MC for Rounds 3, 4, and 5. Various combinations of the A and B yarns are used for Rounds 1 and 2. The following list gives the A and B combinations and specifies how many triangles to make in each colorway.

Bright pink petals (B) with pale pink center (A): 14
Bright pink petals (B) with gold center (A): 15
Bright pink petals (B) with green center (A): 10
Pale pink petals (B) with bright pink center (A): 10
Pale pink petals (B) with gold center (A): 11
Pale pink petals (B) with green center (A): 12
Gold petals (B) with bright pink center (A): 9
Gold petals (B) with pale pink center (A): 10
Gold petals (B) with green center (A): 11
Green petals (B) with bright pink center (A): 11
Green petals (B) with pale pink center (A): 12
Green petals (B) with gold center (A): 11

Blanket layout

TIP

When you have made all the triangles for the blanket you will be eager to get them joined and the project finished. But these motifs, especially if made using a silk yarn, may be a little out of shape so it's important to sew in all the ends first, then block and steam each triangle on the wrong side before laying out the blanket design.

To make the blanket

(Make a total of 136 triangles)

Foundation ring: Using A, make 4ch and join in with a ss in first ch to form a ring.

Round 1 (RS): 5ch (counts as 1dc and 3ch), *[1dc in ring, 2ch] 5 times, join with a ss in 3rd of 5-ch at beg of round. Fasten off A.

Cont in rounds with RS always facing you.

Round 2: Join B with a ss in top of any dc, *5ch, 3dtrCL in next 2-ch sp, 5ch, 1sc/rf around next dc from previous Round; rep from * 5 times more, join with a ss in same sp as joining st. Fasten off B.

Round 3: Join MC with a ss in top of any 3dtrCL from previous Round, 7ch (counts as 1tr and 3ch), 1tr in same st (corner), *3ch, 1dtr in next sc/rf, 3ch, 1sc in next 3dtrCL, 3ch, 1dtr in next sc/rf, 3ch, [1tr, 3ch, 1tr] (corner) in next 3dtrCL; rep from * once more, 3ch, 1dtr in next sc/rf, 3ch, 1sc in next 3dtrCL, 3ch, 1dtr in next sc/rf, 3ch, join with a ss in 4th of first 7-ch.

Round 4: Ss in next 3-ch sp, 6ch, (counts as 1dc and 3ch), 2dc in same ch sp (corner), *[1dc in next st, 3dc in next ch sp] 4 times**, 1dc in next st, [2dc, 3ch, 2dc] in corner sp*; rep from * to * once more, then work from * to **, 1dc in same place as ss at end of Round 3, 1dc in same sp as ss at beg of round, join with a ss in 3rd of first 6-ch. *21 dc on each side of triangle.*

Round 5: Ss in next 3-ch sp, 6ch (counts as 1dc and 3ch), 2dc in same ch sp (corner), *1dc in each dc to next corner sp, [2dc, 3ch, 2dc] in corner sp; rep from * once more, 1dc in each dc to next corner, 1dc in same place as ss at end of Round 4, 1dc in same corner sp as ss at beg of round, join with a ss in third of first 6-ch. *25 dc on each side of triangle.*

Fasten off.

To finish the blanket

Lay out all the triangles on a flat surface, making sure that you place the colors randomly and evenly setting them out in strips as in the diagram.

Join the triangles together in strips using the overcast method (see Workshop 2, Joining squares: Overcast method, page 37) with right sides together.

Triangle motif chart

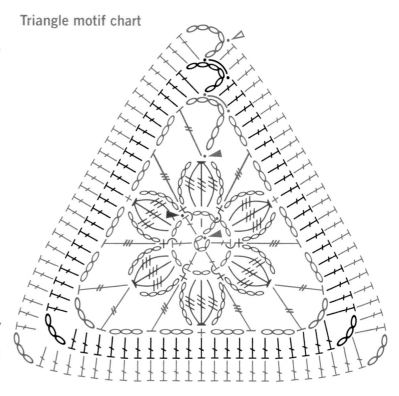

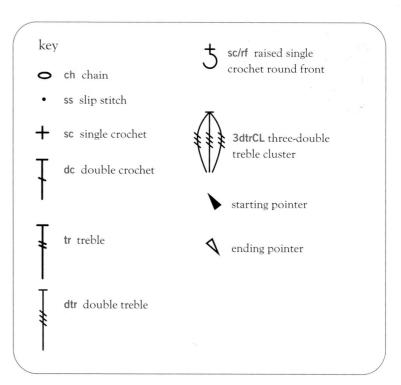

key

⬭ **ch** chain

• **ss** slip stitch

+ **sc** single crochet

† **dc** double crochet

╪ **tr** treble

‡ **dtr** double treble

⌇ **sc/rf** raised single crochet round front

◇ **3dtrCL** three-double treble cluster

◣ starting pointer

◁ ending pointer

Workshop 19

Raised flowers

Raised flowers are flowers that stand up from the surface of the crochet to create a 3-D effect. Raised flowers are made by crocheting into the back of the petals (from the previous round) and making loops. In the following round the loops are crocheted into, using the stitches to create the petal shapes. The project in this Workshop, the Corsage, will allow you to put this technique into practice. This Workshop also explains the difference between clusters, bobbles, and popcorns.

Making a raised flower

Using MC, 5ch, join with a ss in first ch to form a ring.

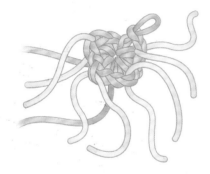

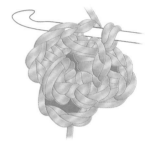

Round 1 (RS): *1sc, 1dc, 1sc in ring; rep from * 3 times more.
4 petals.
At the start of the flower and after this round, it's quite difficult to see where the petals are. Try putting stitch markers in the top of each of the four double crochet, so you can see the where the petals are. Do not join this yarn, it's the center of the flower.

Hold the work with the right side facing you, then turn your hand to look at the back of the work. Insert the hook into the back loops of the single crochet after the double crochet (where the stitch holder is).
Round 2: *2ch, working from WS, 1ss in base of 2nd sc of next petal (pick up 2 loops); rep from * 3 times more (4 loops).

Make 2ch, and repeat from * again until 3 loops have been made, make another 2ch and ss into the back of the last sc of Round 1.

Yarn over hook, pull the yarn though to slip stitch through the single crochet loops and the loop on the hook.

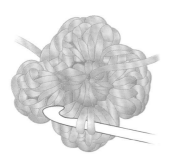 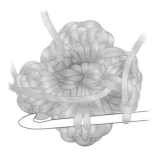

Round 3: *4dc in next 2-ch sp (at back), 1ss into same ch sp; rep from * 3 more times. Fasten off.
Continue working with MC. Work into the back of the petals picking up two loops.
Join MC with a ss at the base of the highest point of first petal of the previous round (in center of petal—at back).
Round 3 is the first round of making the petals, which will be made into the loops (chain spaces) that have just been created in Round 2. The yarn is fastened off on this round but you will continue to use the same color in the next round. This is so that the petals are placed in the next round in between the petals made in this round.

*3ch, 1ss in center of base of the next petal; rep from * twice more, 3ch, join with a ss in joining ss at beginning of round.
Round 5: *8dc into next 3-ch sp, 1ss in same 3-ch sp; rep from * 3 times more.
Fasten off.

These are the loops that are the base for the leaves, which are worked in the same way as the petals in the previous rounds.
Change to B. Working into back of petals and picking up two loops at the back of the st as follows, join yarn with a ss in center of base of first petal (next 8-dc group) of previous round.
Round 6: *3ch, 1ss in center of base of the next petal; rep from * twice more, 3ch, join with a ss in joining ss at beg of round.
Round 7: Continue using B, *10dc in first 3ch sp, 1ss in same 3-ch sp; rep from * 3 times more.
Fasten off.

*3ch, 1ss in center of base of the next petal; rep from * twice more, 3ch, join with a ss in joining ss at beginning of round.
Round 4: Continue working with MC. Working into the back of the petals and picking up two loops at the back of st, join MC with a ss at the base of the highest point of the first petal of the previous round (in center of petal—at back).

Raised flower chart

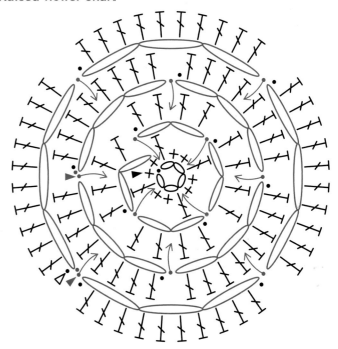

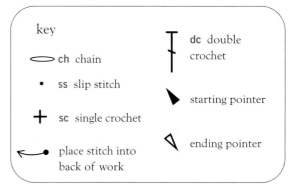

Clusters, Bobbles, and Popcorns

These all create lovely textured shapes that stand out in relief. Clusters are a series of partial stitches, each created in one of the following stitches in the round or row, and then joined together at the top. Decreases are a form of cluster and can often be called clusters if they are followed by increases to form different textured shapes in the pattern.

Bobbles are created by making partial stitches all into the same stitch (or space) and then joining them all together at the top by completing the stitch being worked, sometimes with the addition of a chain (this depends on the pattern).

five-double crochet cluster (5dcCL) in symbols

Popcorns are a series of complete stitches all made into one stitch or space, which are then drawn together by taking the crochet hook out of the loop of the last stitch in the sequence, inserting it at the beginning of the group and then back into the loop of the last stitch. The yarn is then pulled through to create the popcorn. Please see below the steps to make a popcorn.

five-double crochet popcorn (5-dc Popcorn) in symbols

Popcorn

This example shows a popcorn made with four double crochet stitches worked into a foundation chain, but a popcorn can be worked into any stitch or space and can be made up of any practical number or combination of stitches.

1 Inserting the hook in the same place each time, work four complete double crochet.

2 Slip the hook out of the last loop and insert it into the top of the first stitch.

3 Then insert the hook into the loop of the last stitch again. yarn over hook and pull it through as indicated.

4 This makes one complete popcorn.

five-double crochet popcorn (5-dc Popcorn) in symbols

Corsages

These corsages can be made using up scraps of yarn in any light worsted (DK) or worsted (Aran) weight yarn. I've often used this pattern to make decorations for my presents too—just attach the piece to a narrow ribbon to make a unique gift wrap embellishment.

techniques used

Stitches—single crochet, double crochet

Making a flower corsage

yarns

Rooster *Almerino Aran* (50% baby alpaca, 50% merino wool) Aran-(worsted-) weight yarn

Debbie Bliss *Rialto DK* (100% extra-fine merino wool superwash) double-knitting-weight yarn

Lilac flower:
Small amount of Rooster *Almerino Aran* in main color:
MC 319 Lilac Sky

Dark pink flower:
Small amount of Debbie Bliss *Rialto DK* in main color:
MC 50 Deep Rose

Pale pink flower:
Small amount of Debbie Bliss *Rialto DK* in main color:
MC 42 Pink

Yellow flower:
Small amount of Debbie Bliss *Rialto DK* in main color:
MC 57 Banana

Orange flower:
Small amount of Rooster *Almerino Aran* in main color:
MC 318 Coral

Leaves:
Small amount of Debbie Bliss Rialto DK in leaf color:
A 09 Apple

hook

US size 7 (4.5 mm) crochet hook

extras

Felt circle, approximately 1½ in. (4 cm) in diameter for each corsage, and matching thread
Brooch backing pin, approximately 1 in. (2.5 cm) long

gauge

Gauge is not critical in this project.

abbreviations

ch	chain
dc	double crochet
RS	right side
sc	single crochet
sp(s)	space(s)
ss	slip stitch
st(s)	stitch(es)

To make the corsage

All the corsages are made in the same way, using the same color (A) for the leaves (Rounds 6 and 7) and one of the main colors (MC) for the flower (Rounds 1–5).

Foundation ring: Using MC, work 5ch and join with a ss in first ch to form a ring.

Round 1 (RS): *1sc, 1dc, 1sc in ring; rep from * 3 times more. *4 petals.*

Cont in rounds with RS always facing you and always working behind petals of previous round.

Round 2: *2ch, working from WS work 1ss into base of 2nd sc of next petal (pick up 2 loops); rep from * 3 times more (4 loops).

Round 3: *4dc in next 2-ch sp (at back), 1ss into same ch sp; rep from * 3 times more.

Fasten off.

Continue working with MC.

Round 4: Working into the back of petals and picking up two loops at the back of the st, join MC with a ss at base of highest point of first petal of previous round (in center of petal—at back), *3ch, 1ss in center of base of the next petal; rep from * twice more, 3ch, join with a ss in joining ss at beginning of round.

Round 5: *8dc in next 3-ch sp, 1ss in same 3-ch sp; rep from * 3 times more.

Fasten off.

Change to A.

Working into back of petals and picking up two loops at the back of the st as follows, join yarn with a ss into middle of base of petal (next 8-dc group) of previous round.

Round 6: *3ch, 1ss in center of base of the next petal; rep from * twice more, 3ch, join with a ss in joining ss at beg of round.

Continue using A.

Round 7: *10dc in first 3ch sp, 1ss in same 3-ch sp; rep from * 3 times more.

Fasten off.

To finish the corsage

Using a yarn sewing needle, sew in any yarn ends.

Cut a circle of felt and pin it to the back of the corsage. Using a hand sewing needle and thread, and using a whipping stitch sew the felt circle in place.

Sew a brooch backing pin to the felt.

Raised flower chart

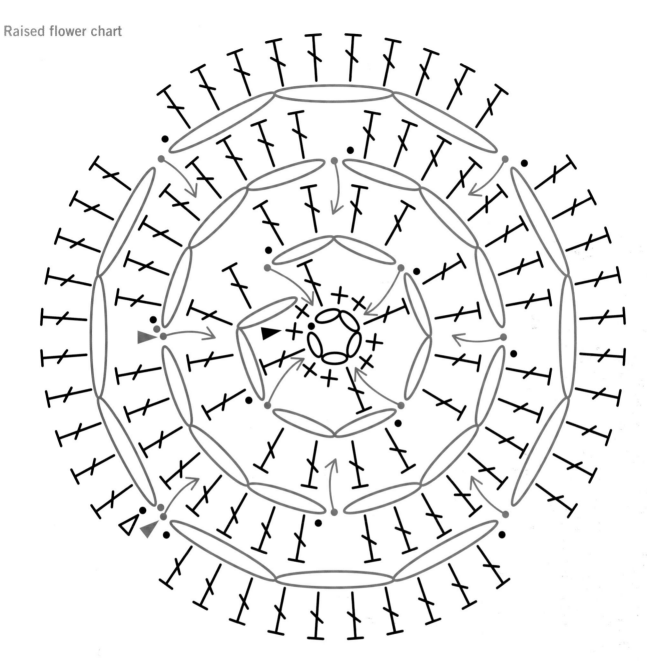

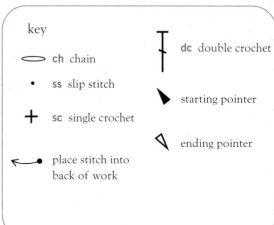

key

⬯ **ch** chain

• **ss** slip stitch

✛ **sc** single crochet

↩• place stitch into
back of work

╈ **dc** double crochet

▶ starting pointer

▷ ending pointer

TIP
To make the back of the flower more
solid, stuff a little yarn behind the felt
before sewing in place.

Workshop 20

Pattern reading practice

Reading patterns is all about practice. Some patterns are written out in different ways, not all spell everything out in fine detail. You may have found a vintage pattern that you'd like to make, using some of the new soft yarns, so it's good to get some practice on what is understood by increases and decreases. This Workshop also covers single crocheting three stitches together (sc3tog) and Shell stitch, which is used for the Camisole project at the end of the Workshop.

Pattern reading practice

In the Silky Camisole project for this Workshop, you'll be working in a fine lace yarn, which is a challenge in itself. Do not expect to work quickly in this yarn as it's fine and the hook size is small. Fine yarns are often on hanks instead of in balls so you will probably have to spend your first evening just concentrating on winding the yarn into balls from the hank.

First choose the right size you'd like to make. If possible photocopy the pattern, read through the whole pattern and either circle or highlight the size that applies to the size you are making. Start on the pattern in the order that it's written. Check that you understand all the techniques and terms in the pattern and if you're not familiar with them, practice them first using a thicker yarn and larger size crochet hook.

The Camisole is mostly made using the simple stitch of single crochet and has a pretty shell stitch on the yoke, edged with a 4-ch picot. The 4-ch picot is described in detail opposite, then just follow the instructions in the pattern. For more information on how to make picots see Workshop 11, Picot, page 98. This pattern uses single and double asterisks (*), standard brackets and will also indicate which is a DEC (decrease) row and which an INC (increase) row.

Single crochet three stitches together (sc3tog)

This stitch is a decrease that takes three stitches down to one stitch.

1 Insert the hook in the st, yarn over hook, pull the yarn through the work (2 loops on hook).

2 Insert the hook in the next st, yarn over hook, pull the yarn through the work (3 loops on hook).

3 Insert the hook in the next st, yarn over hook, pull the yarn though the work (4 loops on hook).

4 Yarn over hook, pull the yarn through all 4 loops on the hook (1 loop on hook). One single crochet three together made.

 single crochet three stitches together (sc3tog) in symbols

Four-chain picot (4-ch picot)

Most picots are 3-ch picots, but to make a bigger "knobble" at an edging you can also make a 4-ch picot. This is based on the same principle as a 3-ch picot but with 4 chains instead of 3.

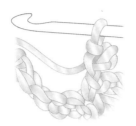

Make 15ch, 1sc in 2nd ch from hook, 1sc in each ch to end.
Next row (picot edging): 1ch, 1sc in first sc, *4ch, ss in 4th ch from hook.

One picot made.

Skip 1 sc, 1sc in next sc; rep from * along edge.
Fasten off.

Solid shell stitch

A shell stitch is a group of a number of stitches in one place. This is a simple stitch and you can see the shapes well on the chart.

Multiples of 6 + 1 stitch.

Make 20ch.
Row 1 (RS): 1ch, 1sc in first st, *skip 2 sts, 5dc in next st, skip 2 sts, 1sc in next st (1 shell made); rep from * twice more ending last rep with 1sc in top of tch, turn.
Row 2: 3ch (counts as 1dc), 2dc in first st, *skip 2 dc, 1sc in next dc, skip 2 dc, 5dc in next sc; rep from * to last 6 sts, skip 2 dc, 1sc in next dc, skip 2 dc, 3dc in last sc, turn.
Rep last 2 rows to form pattern.

Solid shell stitch chart

key

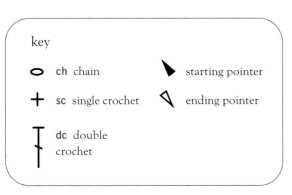

ch chain		starting pointer	
sc single crochet		ending pointer	
dc double crochet			

Silky camisole

A soft silk yarn is perfect for this camisole, which is ideal for summer days or to add a touch of luxury under a jumper in the winter. Once you have made one of these, you will want to make lots in different colors.

To make the camisole front
**Foundation chain: Using a US size C-2 (2.5 mm) hook and MC, make 107(115:121:129:137:143)ch.
Foundation row
Row 1 (RS): 1sc in 2nd ch from hook, 1sc in each ch to end.
106(114:120:128:136:142) sc.
Main body
Next row: 1ch (does not count as a st), 1sc in each sc to end.
This last row forms sc fabric, rep throughout.

Cut off yarn. Join in A.
Next row: 1ch, 1sc in each sc to end.
Rep last row once more.
Cut off yarn.
Join in MC.
Next row: 1ch, 1sc in each sc to end.
Rep this last row for a further 31(31:35:35:43:43) rows.
Next row (dec) (RS): 1ch, 1sc in each of first 12 sc, sc2tog over next 2 sts, 1sc in each sc to last 14 sc, sc2tog over next 2 sts,

techniques used

Stitches—single crochet, double crochet

Working with fine yarn

Shaping bodice, neck and armholes

Making a picot edging

measurements

To fit women's sizes:

| 8 | 10 | 12 | 14 | 16 | 18 |

To fit bust:

| in. | 32 | 34 | 36 | 38 | 40 | 42 |
| cm | 81 | 86 | 91 | 97 | 102 | 107 |

camisole sizes

Around bust

| in. | 30 | 32 | 34 | 36 | 38 | 40 |
| cm | 76 | 81 | 86 | 91 | 97 | 102 |

Approx. length, including strap

| in. | 21 | 21 | 23¼ | 23½ | 24¼ | 24¼ |
| cm | 53 | 53 | 59 | 60 | 63 | 63 |

yarns

Fyberspates *Scrumptious Lace* (55% merino, 45% silk) lace-weight yarn 1(1:2:2:2:2) x 3½oz (100g) hanks—approx. 1094(1094:2188:2188:2188:2188)yd/ 1000(1000:2000:2000:2000:2000)m— of main color:
MC 509 Rose Pink

⁵⁄₁₆(⁵⁄₁₆:⅓:⅓:⅜:⅜)oz/9(9:10:10:11:11)g— approx. 98(98:109:109:120:120)yd/ 90(90:100:100:110:110)m—of a contrasting color:
A 503 Oyster

hooks

US size B-1 (2 mm) crochet hook
US size C-2 (2.5 mm) crochet hook

gauge

28 sts x 44 rows over a 4 in. (10 cm) square worked in single crochet using a US size C-2 (2.5 mm) crochet hook. 6 patt and 1 stitch (37 sts) x 22 rows over a 4 in. (10 cm) square worked shell patt (yoke) using a US size B-1 (2 mm) crochet hook.

abbreviations

ch	chain
cont	continu(e)(ing)
dec	decrease
dc	double crochet
foll	following
hdc	half double crochet
inc	increase
MC	main color
patt	pattern
rep	repeat
RS	right side
sc	single crochet
ss	slip stitch
st(s)	stitch(es)
tch	turning chain
tog	together
WS	wrong side
yoh	yarn over hook

special abbreviations

sc2tog (single crochet 2 together decrease): [Insert hook in next st, yoh and pull yarn through work] twice (3 loops now on hook), yoh and pull through all 3 loops on hook to complete the sc2tog decrease.

sc3tog (single crochet 3 together decrease): [Insert hook in next st, yoh, pull yarn through work] 3 times (4 loops now on hook), yoh, pull yarn through all 4 loops on hook to complete the sc3tog decrease (decreases 2 stitches).

dc2tog (double crochet 2 together decrease): Yoh, insert hook in next st, yoh, pull yarn through work, yoh, pull yarn through first 2 loops on hook (2 loops now on hook), yoh, insert hook in next st, yoh, pull yarn through work, yoh, pull yarn through first 2 loops on hook (3 loops now on hook), yoh, pull yarn through all 3 loops on hook to complete the dc2tog decrease.

1sc in each sc to end.

Work 5 rows in sc.

Rep last 6 rows twice more then dec row once more.
98(106:112:120:128:134) sc.

Work straight for 13 rows.

Next row (inc) (RS): 1ch, 1sc in each of first 12 sc, 2sc in next sc, 1sc in each sc to last 13 sc, 2sc in next sc, 1sc in each sc to end.

Work 5 rows in sc.

Rep last 6 rows twice more then inc row once more.
106(114:120:128:136:142) sc.

Work straight until body measures 11(11:12:12:13:13) in./
28(28:31:31:33:33) cm.

Cut off yarn. Join in A.

Next row: 1ch, 1sc in each sc to end.

Rep last row once more.

Cut off yarn. Join in MC.

Next row: 1ch, 1sc in each sc to end.

Change to US size B-1 (2 mm) crochet hook.

Next row (inc) (RS): 1ch, 1sc in each of first 13(11:6:4:2:21) sc, *2sc in next sc, 1sc in each of next 2(2:2:2:2:1) sc; rep from * 25(29:35:39:43:49) times more, 2sc in next sc, 1sc in each of last 14(12:5:3:1:20) sc. *133(145:157:169:181:193) sc.*

Solid shell stitch chart

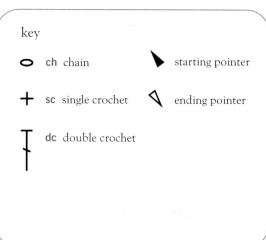

key

- ⟳ **ch** chain
- ✚ **sc** single crochet
- ⊤ **dc** double crochet
- ▶ starting pointer
- ◁ ending pointer

Yoke

Row 1 (RS): 1ch, 1sc in first st, *skip 2 sts, 5dc in next st, skip 2 sts, 1sc in next st (1 shell made); rep from * ending last rep with 1sc in top of tch, turn. *22(24:26:28:30:32) shells.*

Row 2: 3ch (counts as 1dc), 2dc in first st, *skip 2 dc, 1sc in next dc, skip 2 dc, 5dc in next sc; rep from * to last 6 sts, skip 2 dc, 1sc in next dc, skip 2 dc, 3dc in last sc, turn.

These last 2 rows form patt, rep throughout.

Work 4(4:6:6:8:8) more rows in patt, so ending with a WS row.**

Note: 3dc at each end of a row is classed as a half shell.

Left cup shaping

Row 1 (dec) (RS): 1ch, 1sc in first st, *skip 2 dc, 5dc in next sc, skip 2 dc, 1sc in next dc; rep from * 9(10:11:12:13:14) times more, skip 2 dc, 2dc in next sc, skip 2 sts, 1dc in next dc, turn. *10½(11½:12½:13½:14½:15½) shells.*

Row 2: 3ch (counts as 1dc), 4dc in first sc, *skip 2 dc, 1sc in next dc, skip 2 dc, 5dc in next sc; rep from * ending last rep with 3dc in last sc.

Row 3 (dec): 1ch, 1sc in first st, *skip 2 dc, 5dc in next sc, skip 2 dc, 1sc in next st; rep from * to last 8 sts, skip 2 dc, 5dc in next sc, skip 4 sts, 1sc in top of tch of previous row. *10(11:12:13:14:15) shells.*

Row 4: 3ch (counts as 1dc), 2dc in first sc, *skip 2 dc, 1sc in next dc, skip 2 dc, 5dc in next sc; rep from * ending last rep with 3dc in last sc.

Row 5 (dec): 1ch, 1sc in first st, *skip 2 dc, 5dc in next sc, skip 2 dc, 1sc in next dc; rep from * to last 6 sts, skip 2 dc, 2dc in next sc, skip 2 dc, 1dc in top of tch of previous row. *9½(10½:11½:12½:13½:14½) shells.*

Row 6: 1ch, 1sc in first st, skip 2 dc, 5dc in next sc, *skip 2 dc, 1sc in next dc, skip 2 dc, 5dc in next sc; rep from * ending last rep with 3dc in last sc.

Row 7 (dec): 1ch, 1sc in first st, *skip 2 dc, 5dc in next sc, skip 2 dc, 1sc in next dc; rep from * to last 3 sts, skip 2 dc, 1dc in next sc. *9(10:11:12:13:14) shells.*

Rows 8–10: Rep rows 4–6. *8½(9½:10½:11½:12½:13½) shells.*

Armhole and cup shaping

Next row (RS): Ss across first 6 sts, 1sc in next dc, patt across row to last 3 sts, 1dc in next sc. *7(8:9:10:11:12) shells.*

Next row: 3ch (counts as 1dc), 2dc in first sc, skip 2 dc, 1sc in next sc, patt across row to last 3 sts, turn. *6½(7½:8½:9½:10½:11½) shells.*

SIZES 8, 10, 12 and 14 ONLY

Next row (RS): Ss across first 3 sts, 1sc in next dc, patt across row to last 6 sts, skip 2 dc, 2dc in next sc, 1dc in top of tch of previous row. *5½(6½:7½:8½:—:—) shells.*

Next row: 1ch, 1sc in first st, skip 2 dc, 5dc in next sc, skip 2 dc, 1sc in next dc, patt across row to last 3 sts, turn. *5(6:7:8:—:—) shells.*

Next row: Ss across first 3 sts, 1sc in next dc, skip 2 dc, 5dc in next sc, skip 2 dc, 1sc in next dc, patt across row to last 3 sts, 1dc in next sc. *4(5:6:7:—:—) shells.*

SIZES 8 and 12 ONLY

Working straight at armhole edge and starting with Row 4 of cup shaping, continue to dec 3 sts at left cup edge by repeating Rows 4–7 until 3(—:5:—:—:—) shells remain.

SIZES 16 and 18 ONLY

Next row (RS): Ss across first 3 sts, 1sc in next dc, patt across row to last 6 sts, skip 2 sts, dc2tog working first "leg" in next st, skip 1 st and work 2nd "leg" in next st (do not count this st). *–(–:–:–:9:10) shells.*

Next row: 1ch, skip dc2tog of previous row, patt across row to last 3 sts. *–(–:–:–:8½:9½) shells.*

Next row: Ss across first 3 sts, patt across row to last 6 sts, skip 2 sts, dc2tog working first "leg" in next st, skip 1 st and work 2nd "leg" in next st (do not count this st). *–(–:–:–:7:8) shells.*

ALL SIZES

Next row (WS): Rep Row 4.

Next row: 1ch, 1sc in first st, patt across row to last 6 sts, skip 2 sts, dc2tog working first "leg" in next st, skip 1 st, work 2nd "leg" in next st (do not count this st). *2(4:4:6:6:7) shells.*

Rep these last 2 rows 1(3:3:5:5:6) times more. 1 shell (all sizes).

Next row: 3ch (counts as 1dc), 2dc in first sc, skip 2 dc, 1sc in next dc, skip 2 dc, 3dc in last sc.

Strap

Next row (RS): 1ch (do not count as a st), 1sc in each st to end. *7 sc.*

Rep last row until strap measures 4¼(4¼:4¼:4¾:4¾:4¾) in./ 11(11:11:12:12:12) cm or to desired length, ending with a RS row. Fasten off.

Right cup shaping

With RS facing and using a US size B-1 (2 mm) hook and MC, rejoin yarn with a ss to center dc on center shell (same place as last st of first row of Left Cup).

Row 1 (dec) (RS): 3ch, skip 2 dc, 2dc in next sc, skip 2 dc, 1sc in next dc, *skip 2 dc, 5dc in next sc, skip 2 dc, 1sc in next dc; rep from * ending last rep with 1sc in top of tch. *10½(11½:12½:13½:14½:15½) shells.*

Row 2: 3ch (counts as 1dc), 2dc in first sc, *skip 2 dc, 1sc in next dc, skip 2 dc, 5dc in next sc; rep from * to last 6 sts, skip 2 sts, 3dc in next sc, 1dc in top of tch.

Row 3 (dec): 1ch, 1sc in first dc, skip 3 sts, 5dc in next sc, skip 2 dc, 1sc in next dc, * skip 2 dc, 5dc in next sc, skip 2 dc, 1sc in next dc; rep from * ending last rep with 1sc in top of tch. *10(11:12:13:14:15) shells.*

Row 4: 3ch (counts as 1dc), 2dc in first st, *skip 2 dc, 1sc in next dc, skip 2 dc, 5dc in next sc; rep from * to last 6 sts, skip 2 dc, 1sc in next dc, skip 2 dc, 3dc in last sc.

Row 5 (dec): 3ch (counts as 1dc), skip 3 dc, 2dc in next sc, skip 2 dc, 1sc in next dc, *skip 2 dc, 5dc in next sc, skip 2 dc, 1sc in next dc; rep from * ending last rep with 1sc in top of tch. *9½(10½:11½:12½:13½:14½) shells.*

Row 6: 3ch (counts as 1dc), 2dc in first st, *skip 2 dc, 1sc in next dc, skip 2 dc, 5dc in next sc; rep from * to last 3 sts, 1sc in top of tch of previous row.

Row 7 (dec): 3ch (do not count st), skip 2 dc, 1sc in next dc, *skip 2 dc, 5dc in next sc, skip 2 dc, 1sc in next dc; rep from * ending last rep with 1sc in top of tch. *9(10:11:12:13:14) shells.*

Rows 8–10: Rep rows 4–6. *8½(9½:10½:11½:12½:13½) shells.*

Armhole and cup shaping

Next row (RS): 3ch (do not count as a st), skip 2 dc, 1sc in next dc, *skip 2 dc, 5dc in next sc, skip 2 dc, 1sc in next dc; rep from * to last 6 sts, turn. *7(8:9:10:11:12) shells.*

Next row: Ss across first 3 sts, 1sc in next st, *skip 2 dc, 5dc in next sc, skip 2 dc, 1sc in next dc; rep from * to last 3 sts, skip 2 dc, 3dc in last sc. *6½(7½:8½:9½:10½:11½) shells.*

SIZES 8, 10, 12 and 14 ONLY

Next row (RS): 3ch (counts as 1dc), skip 3 dc, 2dc in next sc, skip 2 dc, 1sc in next dc, *skip 2 dc, 5dc in next sc, skip 2 dc, 1sc in next dc; rep from * to last 3 sts, turn. *5½(6½:7½:8½–:–) shells.*

Next row: Ss across first 3 sts, 1sc in next st, skip 2 dc, 5dc in next sc, skip 2 dc, patt across row to end, ending last rep with 1sc in top of tch. *5(6:7:8:–:–) shells.*

Next row: 3ch (do not count st), skip 2 dc, 1sc in next dc, *skip 2 dc, 5dc in next sc, skip 2 dc, 1sc in next dc; rep from * to last 3 sts, turn. *4(5:6:7:–:–) shells.*

SIZES 8 and 12 ONLY

Working straight at armhole edge and starting with row 4 of cup shaping, continue to dec 3 sts at right cup edge by repeating Rows 4–7 until 3(–:5:–:–:–) shells remain.

SIZES 16 and 18 ONLY

Next row (RS): [3ch (counts as 1dc), skip 3 dc, 1dc in next sc] (do not count these sts), skip 2 dc, 1sc in next dc, skip 2 dc, 5dc in next sc, patt across row to last 3 sts, turn. *–(–:–:–:9:10) shells.*

Next row: Patt across row to last 3 sts, turn. *–(–:–:–:8½:9½) shells.*

Next row: [3ch (counts as 1dc), 1dc in next sc] (do not count these sts), skip 2 dc, 1sc in next dc, skip 2 dc, 5dc in next sc, patt across row to last 3 sts, turn. *–(–:–:–:7:8) shells.*

ALL SIZES

Next row (WS): Rep Row 4 ending with 2dc in last sc, 1dc in top of tch of previous row.

Next row: [3ch (counts as 1dc), skip 3 dc, 1dc in next sc] (do not count these sts), skip 2 dc, 1sc in next dc, skip 2 dc, 5dc in next sc, patt across row to end. *2(4:4:6:6:7) shells.*

Rep last 2 rows 1(3:3:5:5:6) times more. *1 shell (all sizes).*

Next row: 3ch (counts as 1dc), 2dc in first sc, skip 2 dc, 1sc in next dc, skip 2 dc, 3dc in last sc.

Strap

Next row (RS): 1ch (does not count as a st), 1sc in each st to end. *7 sc.*

Rep last row until strap measures 4¼(4¼:4¼:4¾:4¾:4¾) in./ 11(11:11:12:12:12) cm or to your desired length, ending with a RS row.

To make the camisole back

Work as for Front from ** to **.

Work a further 10(10:10:10:10:10) rows straight, so ending with a WS row.

Armhole shaping

Row 1 (RS): Ss across first 6 sts, 1sc in next st, skip 2 dc, 5dc in next sc, patt across row to last 6 sts, turn. *20(22:24:26:28:30) shells.*

Left back strap

With RS facing and using a US size B-1 (2 mm) hook and MC, rejoin yarn with a ss to 7th st in from left back side edge, 1ch, 1sc in same place as ss, 1sc in each st to end, turn. *7 sc.*

Work from * to * as for right back strap.

To join the front and back together

Join right front and right back straps together by placing both right sides together, rejoin yarn to right edge using a US size B-1 (2 mm) hook and MC, insert the hook from front to back through the edges of both straps, yoh and pull yarn through, work 1sc in the usual way, then insert the hook in the next stitch along ready to make next sc. Continue along the strap until all the sc have been joined together. Fasten off.

Rep with both left front and left back straps.

Using a yarn sewing needle, join side seams.

To work the lower edging

With RS facing and using a 2mm (US size B-1) hook and A, rejoin yarn to left back side edge, 1ch, work 1 row of sc evenly around lower edge, ending by joining with a ss in first sc of round (working enough sc to be a multiple of 2), turn.

Next row: 1ch, 1sc in each sc to end of round, join with a ss in first sc of round, turn.

Next row (picot edging): 1ch, 1sc in first sc, *4ch, 1ss in 4th ch from hook (picot made), skip 1 sc, 1sc in next sc; rep from * skipping last sc in last rep, join with a ss in first sc of round. Fasten off.

To work the top front edging

With RS facing and using a 2mm (US size B-1) hook and A, rejoin yarn to start of left front strap, 1ch, work 1 row of sc down left cup, then up right cup to start of strap working sc3tog in center front with 1 "leg" in left cup, 1 "leg" in center and 1 "leg" in right cup (making the sc a multiple of 2 plus 1), turn.

Next row: 1ch, 2sc in first sc, 1sc in each sc working sc3tog over center 3 sts as for last row, ending with 2sc in last sc, turn.

Next row (picot edging): 1ch, 1sc in first sc, *4ch, 1ss in 4th ch from hook (picot made), skip 1 sc, 1sc in next sc; rep from * to end, working sc3tog over center 3 sts as for last row.

Fasten off.

Sew row ends of edging to side edge of strap.

To work the top back edging

With RS facing and using a US size B-1 (2 mm) hook and A, rejoin yarn to right back top edge where it meets strap, 1ch, work 1 row of sc along top edge to left back strap edge (making the sc a multiple of 2 plus 1), turn.

Next row: 1ch, 1sc in each sc to end, turn.

Next row (picot edging): 1ch, 1sc in first sc, *4ch, 1ss in 4th ch from hook (picot made), skip 1 sc, 1sc in next sc; rep from * to end. Fasten off.

Sew row ends of edging to side edge of straps.

Row 2: Ss across first 3 sts, 1sc in next st, skip 2 dc, 5dc in next sc, skip 2 dc, 1sc in next dc, patt across row to last 3 sts, turn. *19(21:23:25:27:29) shells.*

Rep last row 3 times more. *16(18:20:22:24:26) shells.*

Keeping patt correct, work straight until same number of rows have been worked as for Front to start of front strap, ending with a WS row.

Next row (RS): 1ch, 1sc in each of first 2 dc, *1hdc in next dc, 1dc in next sc, 1hdc in next dc, 1sc in each of next 3 dc; rep from *, ending last rep with 1sc in each of last 2 sts.

Fasten off.

Right back strap

With RS facing and using a 2mm (US size B-1) hook and MC, rejoin yarn with a ss to first st, 1ch, 1sc in same place as ss, 1sc in each of next 6 sts, turn. *7 sc.*

***Next row:** 1ch, 1sc in each sc to end. *7 sc.*

Rep last row until strap measures 4¼(4¼:4¼:4¾:4¾:4¾) in./ 11(11:11:12:12:12) cm or to your desired length, ending with a RS row.

Fasten off.*

Suppliers

US STOCKISTS

Knitting Fever
(Debbie Bliss, Noro, and Sirdar yarns)
Stores nationwide
www.knittingfever.com

The Knitting Garden
(Debbie Bliss, Noro and Sirdar yarns)
www.theknittinggarden.com

Webs
(yarn, crochet hooks, accessories, tuition)
75 Service Center Rd
Northampton, MA 01060
1-800-367-9327
www.yarn.com
customerservice@yarn.com

Wool2Dye4
(range of British yarns)
www.wool2dye4.com

Yarn Market
(yarn, crochet hooks, accessories)
12936 Stonecreek Drive, Unit D
Pickerington, OH 43147
1-888-996-9276
www.yarnmarket.com

ACCESSORIES

A.C. Moore
(crochet hooks, accessories)
Online and east coast stores
1-888-226-6673
www.acmoore.com

Hobby Lobby
(crochet hooks, accessories)
Online and stores nationwide
1-800-888-0321
www.hobbylobby.com

Jo-Ann Fabric and Craft Store
(crochet hooks, accessories)
Stores nationwide
1-888-739-4120
www.joann.com

Michaels
(crochet hooks, beads)
Stores nationwide
1-800-642-4235
www.michaels.com

Unicorn Books and Crafts
(crochet hooks, accessories)
1-707-762-3362
www.unicornbooks.com
help@unicornbooks.com

UK STOCKISTS

Laughing Hens
(yarn, crochet hooks, accessories)
The Croft Stables
Station Lane
Great Barrow
Cheshire CH3 7JN
01829 740903
www.laughinghens.com
sales@laughinghens.com

Deramores
(yarn, crochet hooks, accessories)
0800 488 0708 or 01795 668144
www.deramores.com
customer.service@deramores.com

Designer Yarns
(distributor for Debbie Bliss yarns)
www.designeryarns.uk.com

Fyberspates Ltd
(yarn, crochet hooks)
01829 732525
fyberspates@btinternet.com
www.fyberspates.co.uk

Hobbycraft
(yarn, crochet hooks)
Stores nationwide
0330 026 1400
www.hobbycraft.co.uk

John Lewis
(yarn, crochet hooks, accessories)
Stores nationwide
03456 049049 or 01698 545454
www.johnlewis.com

TUITION

Nicki Trench
Crochet Club, workshops, accessories
www.nickitrench.com
nicki@nickitrench.com

ACCESSORIES

Addi Needles
(crochet hooks)
01529 240510
www.addineedles.co.uk
addineedles@yahoo.co.uk

Debbie Abrahams Beads
(beads)
0115 855 1799
www.debbieabrahamsbeads.co.uk
beads@debbieabrahamsbeads.com

Crochet stitch conversion chart

Crochet stitches are worked in the same way in both the US and the UK, but the stitch names are not the same and identical names are used for different stitches. Below is a list with the US terms and the equivalent UK term.

US TERM	UK TERM
single crochet (sc)	double crochet (dc)
half double crochet (hdc)	half treble (htr)
double crochet (dc)	treble (tr)
treble (tr)	double treble (dtr)
double treble (dtr)	triple treble (trtr)
triple treble (trtr)	quadruple treble (qtr)
yarn over hook (yoh)	yarn round hook (yrh)

Index

Acknowledgments

It's been a pleasure to work on this book, but it's very much a team effort. My thanks to all the wonderful and creative people who have helped to make it such a success. They are:

My fantastic team of crocheters: Carolyn Meggison, Jenny Shore, Mitch Bull, Duriye Aydin, Tracey Elks, Emma Lightfoot, Zara Poole, and as always, my Mum, Beryl Oakes.

Our brilliant editorial team and pattern checkers with eyes like hawks: Marie Clayton, Jane Czaja, Sally Harding, Susan Horan, and Emily Davies. Also our illustrators Stephen Dew, Emily Breen, and Kuo Kang Chen and the great team who did such a good job of the photography, styling, and design: James Gardiner, Jo Thornhill, and Barbara Zuniga.

Gillian Haslam from Cico Books deserves a special mention here for her fantastic ability to co-ordinate and pull all the sections of this very comprehensive and detailed book together and her hard work in trying to keep everyone on track. Also big thanks to Sally Powell for the art direction and also to Cindy Richards for commissioning me to write something that felt natural to me. Big thanks to all! I think it's the best crochet "bible" ever!